The Butterfly Within

To, Selina + Jess,

   Keep up the great
   work!

  Best Wishes

     Rachel
        xxx

The

Butterfly

Within

A triathlete's race against

a brain tumour

RACHEL BOWN

Book Guild Publishing

First published in Great Britain in 2016 by
The Book Guild Ltd
9 Priory Business Park
Wistow Road, Kibworth
Leicestershire, LE8 0RX
Freephone: 0800 999 2982
www.bookguild.co.uk
Email: info@bookguild.co.uk
Twitter: @bookguild

Typeset in Baskerville

Printed and bound in Great Britain by
CPI Group (UK) Ltd, Croydon, CR0 4YY

ISBN 978 1 910878 43 9

British Library Cataloguing in Publication Data.
A catalogue record for this book is available from the British Library.

For: Tim, my family, my friends, my wonderful support network and for anyone who has laughed with me or at me along the way!

Thank you to: The Southmead Hospital Neurological Team, Ward 6B and Larkrise School

Prologue

In 2005 I had an epiphany. God smashed His way into my life and since then I have never doubted His love. Then a few months before D-Day (Diagnosis Day) I had an overwhelming calling – I wanted to serve Him. I wanted to be a vicar and I researched how I could train to do this alongside teaching. But I struggled with certain issues. Issues that I could resolve once I had a congregation but would have to bury to reach that point. You see, to get through the selection process I would have to 'tow the religious line' and say what the interviewers wanted to hear. I don't go to church because I don't like the Church as an institution. It makes me feel uncomfortable which obviously seems weird if you want to be a vicar! I also race most Sundays and as I know God wants me to be happy I don't think he would want me to stop this! But I also truly believed that if I was a vicar I could work around these challenges. I could make the Church accessible to others who felt like me and I could be the cool, sporty vicar who ran or cycled to service! However, I knew I couldn't say any of this before I became ordained and so my internal struggle continued.

Then I was diagnosed and my health became my priority, so I put my calling 'on hold' and thought I would reassess my feelings when I was well again. But then pretty much straight away I began to see that my Christian values, my belief system, the strength that underpinned everything I was coping with could reach far more people through me just being me. I didn't need to quote from the Bible for people to listen and in fact more people heard what I was saying because it wasn't overtly religious. My religious values are working, real life values. My biggest Facebook post had over 7000 hits. I could never fit that many people in my church! So you see my faith has underpinned every post written on Facebook and every word you will read in this book. I have never questioned God. I have never asked "why me?" because the answer is clear. God did call to me, but not because He wanted me to wear a dog collar and deliver church services. He knew that because I could cope with what He sent me and because of my personality and my sport I could reach out to many more listeners and be heard. He knew that my parish could never be mapped out in a traditional way. He wanted me to open my church doors and say, "Welcome, my name is Rachel Bown, I am a triathlete and I am going to help you smile and love life!"

Part 1

It's a year since I first visited my GP. I explained something was wrong with my vision but nothing was wrong with my eyes! It's a year since he asked me what I was really worried about and I answered, "A brain tumour."

So you see I knew right from the start. But three GPs later and a visit to the A & E department at my local hospital − no-one listened. It's stress. It might be a migraine. You're tired from training. You haven't got any classic symptoms! You are too fit to be poorly!

Well surprise surprise. A year later and a private visit to see a neurologist. A visit that I had to ask for and the type of specialist I requested − my GP wanted me to see 'the eye man' − I do have a tumour growing behind my right eye.

Apparently it's a benign tumour growing into my brain and pressing on anything in its way! It's now called Tommy and just as a good friend said "Tommy can do one!"

So how do I feel two days after being told my whole world is about to spin out of control for the foreseeable future? Well I'm not sleeping as this 11.45pm laptop stint demonstrates! Bullet points coming up:

1) Totally loved and supported. I have such fab friends and family and of course Tim. I don't feel alone, I feel lucky.

2) I'm terrified of what might happen after my treatment. Will I be different physically and/or mentally? I only know the basics at the moment – that I can't drive or exercise and that I will need radiation therapy and/or an op.

3) Will I be 'me'? My life is so great. I have so much. Will that slip away?

4) I'm exhausted already! Telling everyone is hard. First I see shock. Then sadness and fear. Then they rally themselves to support me and ask questions. I feel their pain no matter how hard they try to hide it.

People have already started saying how brave and inspirational I am. I want to be. I want to be that person who people refer to in that way. I want to be that triathlete who has their comeback race.

And that's what will drive me forwards. Of course staying alive and leading a normal life comes first, but actually running, cycling and swimming is normal for me. That's what I do. Don't get me wrong, I know that Rachel Bown is more than just an athlete. I am a loving daughter, sister, partner, friend. And I am a great teacher. But, what makes me an even better daughter, sister, partner, friend and teacher is being a triathlete. It focuses me. It keeps my work/life balance balanced. It keeps me fresh and gives me the confidence and personal belief that I can do and be anything. I am patient and prepared to persevere. One day I want to be World Champion!

So that's really my circle of life! It worries me that I might have to settle for less and just be grateful to be alive. And then I feel selfish and confused. Obviously I want to stay alive and obviously I don't want my friends and family to suffer, but I can't protect them.

Perhaps I'm just too shocked to think rationally and when this phase subsides I will feel differently? All I know at 00.13am on Saturday 5th July is that I'm tired, tearful and pretty much in denial. I know Tommy is there. I know he's causing trouble. I know he has to come out. But in my 'Rachel Bown is invincible mind' it's just another race! I know this is wrong and probably cheesy and childish but I just see myself winning and everyone saying how amazing I am!

Quite frankly the other scenario is too scary and I am going to continue to push it away. I know I will crack and just as I always do before a big race, I will have doubts. I will feel sorry for myself at some point; several points I should imagine, but then I will refocus, put my plan together and start. The program may have to deviate and be flexible, but fundamentally the finish line will be the same – to start my next race!

I have chosen this photo above all others because it shows every sinew in my body and every bit of my personality reaching for the line. Little did I know that less than two weeks later I would be competing against the most difficult opponent of my life!

PART 2

Most people know now.

Walking into Mum and Dad's yesterday knowing I was about to throw their world up in the air was one of the hardest things I've ever had to do. Mum hasn't been well emotionally for the last 18 months and I knew this would make her nose dive.

It felt terrible watching them trying to absorb the information. The confusion and fear in their eyes. That need to protect me and the helplessness they felt was horrible to see. Mum could hardly breathe and she couldn't speak – we couldn't communicate and sat in silence. So I left them for an hour to cry and be with each other. I walked Murph in the sunshine and felt relieved to be away from the sadness.

When I returned they had rallied themselves and were ready to help me fight. I knew they would, but I also knew they would need a bit of space to do that. It was just too big a shock for them to just jump into action. They didn't even know I had been going for tests, so it was a complete curve ball.

This could be the turning point for Mum. Perhaps she will get some perspective and once she realises she has got the strength to fight for me, she will fight for herself. If God wants me to go through this Hell to make my Mum well, then bring it on! I can cope with this and if in the future we both look at each other and know we are healthy and happy then I will have the answer to the ultimate question – Why me???

I've told the story again and again and still it feels like someone else's story. I haven't cried yet. People say I'm brave and coping well but I'm scared to cry – I may never stop! And also I'm not supposed to raise my blood pressure!

I think my breaking point will be when I see 'Two Ts' on the scan. Oh yeah its name has changed now. Tim kept calling it 'Terry' just to wind me up so I decided Tommy/Terry would become 'Two Ts'. (Two Ts' can still "fuck off!") I think seeing it and discussing my treatment will be the moment it all becomes real and the moment I can't hold it all back. Crying will probably be a good thing. It will signify entering the competition and fully understanding what my opponent's strengths and weaknesses are.

We went to watch the Big Cow Triathlon England Sprint Championships today. Why? It's a long story, but we had to go despite me not racing. I've always said that one of the most important aspects of triathlon has been the friendships I have made and how important they are to me. Today proved this. My triathlon mucker Justine (who I met at the 2010 Worlds in Budapest when she gave me an inner tube) and her partner Big Phil travelled three hours to the race to see me! How amazing is that?! And they brought me 'Edward Bear' to keep me safe during my treatment. Priceless.

Messages of support and comfort have continued to flood in as the news has filtered out. Wow, I know a lot of thoughtful people!

PART 3

A girl at school gave me one of those friendship type band things – you know, the latest craze. All the kids are making them at the moment. She put it on me and said, "You will keep it on won't you Rach?"

I replied, "You have no idea how important this band is to me," and cried a tear inside. I will wear this band every day until it falls off.

My favourite girly couple in the whole wide world have been helping to keep my chin up. Bev and Ali are two of my oldest, dearest friends. I was best woman at their wedding last year – one of the proudest, best days of my life!

They brought me flowers and as always made me laugh. And through their visit 'Two Ts' evolved again!

Tommy/Terry → Two Ts → Tooties

So the tumour is now called 'Tooties'. I feel happy with this. Any Tommies or Terries out there might be upset. Who wants to be thought of as a 'growth'!?

I sorted out my 'Sporting Champions' stuff today. Every year I organise a prize giving assembly. Parents/Carers/Coaches etc are all invited and it's a fabulous celebration of everything the kids achieve in PE throughout the year. I put a slide show together with emotive music (aim – to make people cry!) and award someone from every class. I am determined that this will go ahead in some shape or form. It's such a great afternoon. It takes about an hour, but most of the kids manage to sit and be part of it. It's noisy, interactive and fast moving and I love it! Not sure I will get through it without a few tears this time though, but who cares? I love teaching those kids and want them and their parents to know that!

Someone who I don't usually have much to do with came and gave me her best wishes and said I was an inspiration to the school and should be a motivational speaker when all this is over. I am grateful for her comment and it is something I would like to do, but I did think to myself, "I am inspired every day just working here." It sounds corny, but I can't see how you can work at Larkrise without feeling proud and humbled by the kids. I know my job is to differentiate everything and make it accessible to everyone, but they still have to 'want to do it' and 'give it a try'. And they always do! They always find a way and I think that's what 'inspiration and motivation' look like.

PART 4

I've been to lunch at the House of Lords today and then onto a London hotel for dinner and a conference tomorrow. It's all to do with my PE inclusion work. And

I've laughed. I've been myself. I've had hours where I didn't talk about Tooties and actually periods when it didn't even cross my mind (even if it is still in my head!). I've been really looking forwards to this trip and although I'm annoyed that my treatment plan hasn't been decided yet, at least I've experienced this and being 'me' again for a bit. No-one knows here you see. They don't need to. Not today anyway. When we start the regional planning for next term I will have to say something, but until then I can enjoy being free. One of my colleagues said I was a bad influence – I took it as a compliment!

Part 5

Today has been my lowest day since I had 'the phone call'. I really wanted to buy some new PJs and some nice smellies for my upcoming hospital stay. I could have asked 'hundreds' of friends to accompany me, but I asked my mum. I caught the train to Chippenham and then dad arrived to pick me up – mum wasn't there! She wasn't well enough. So I went to see her. She cried and said she was a terrible mother. Of course I didn't agree but I went to Swindon on my own and spent two lonely hours wandering around wishing she was there. And for the first time I did feel sorry for myself. I do feel sorry for myself today. My mum is too poorly to support me. My dad is too hurt to protect me. Tim is working away. My brother is trying to cope with mum and dad and me. I can't talk to my friends because telling them about mum's depression seems wrong and I don't want anyone to judge her. And what can anyone do anyway? Nothing! Why? Because Mum's illness is as chronic as mine and she can't help it. And so that's where I am. I know realistically Mum won't be able to be at the hospital for me but it doesn't stop me hoping. How will I go down to theatre without her there? How will I wake up without her there? My heart is breaking. I'm frustrated. I know she loves me and would if she could. So I hate her illness because I can only ever love her.

Today has been horrible, but it would have been horrible even if Tooties wasn't here. I hurt inside. I want to cry.

So in racing terms what would this be the equivalent of? My goggles being kicked off? A puncture? What would I do if I punctured mid-race? I would have to continue in some way. I would have to overcome the initial disappointment and then get on with it. I would have a choice. I could sit down and wallow and wait for the sweep vehicle, which could take ages and I wouldn't even get to run. Or I could walk back as fast as possible, see the run as a separate race and collect my finisher's medal. No choice in my head even with the unwanted lodger!

And so tomorrow will be a different day. Mum will still be poorly. Dad and Richard will still be trying to cope. Tim will still be away. But I will be back on top. I'm seeing more friends and have lots to do. I don't really have a choice. As I've said before. There is a big black hole. The Devil is on the edge waiting to push me. He has whispered in my ear today. But I'm not going to listen. I'm in a race and I am never distracted in a race. Well only briefly for photo opportunities and at the moment I can't see a camera worth smiling at!!

PART 6

A lot has happened in three days – a lot!

Mum hit rock bottom and allowed us to step in. She was admitted to hospital yesterday and is already looking and feeling much better. Of course there is a looooong way to go, but she is safe now and in the system. I feel better in myself for knowing that. When I get frustrated I become very unbalanced and I get what Tim calls 'the pinball effect' in my head (and as we know I haven't got enough space for anything else!). This means my thoughts just bounce around and I can't order them. For every positive there is a negative. They fight each other until I find a solution. With Mum it was painful too, because I just felt helpless.

Mixed in with this was my follow-up appointment with the neurologist. Naturally 'Supergirl' here – well I do have PJs and pants confirming that – thought Tooties would be accessible, easily treatable and normal service would resume probably by the end of the summer hols! That's the up/down side of my psyche. One side always looks for the 'worst case scenario' and then works backwards whilst the other side thinks 'I don't have normal rules and stuff just won't apply!'

It was a big shock to see and hear how big it is and how damaging it is becoming. It's pushing on my temporal lobe, pituitary gland, eye and nasal passage. Yes my nose! My nose. Bizarrely this fact is really bothering me! Perhaps it's because I pick my nose a lot and am scared I might find it?! Anyway I cried a bit for the first time. It didn't last long but it was pretty heavy. I won't be able to drive for at least a year and the recovery period is a minimum of three months. "I don't believe I will ever be back to how I was in Austria" – that's the chimp talking. "I'm going to take my time and come back better than ever. I will be World Champion one day" – that's me talking. It's so hard sitting here facing the unknown feeling pretty OK, knowing that for a period I will feel like shit and then have to start all over again!

PART 7

It really is the thoughts and gestures that matter. Of course I love presents – lots of presents, but sometimes something unexpected happens and it has a massive impact. An impact that the person who showed the kindness may never know. Tiree's funeral was yesterday. She was a beautiful, innocent 18 year old girl who loved pink! Saying goodbye to her and seeing her parent's pain was tragic. The church and crematorium were packed. Some students attended and one girl who I have taught for ten years wanted to sit by me and her class teacher. I cried. I tried not to but the tears just came. And this lovely girl turned to me and wiped my tears – priceless. And that's why I do it. That's why I teach these fabulous children with nothing but love in their hearts and that's why I am still going to work every day. I believe there really is a professional, appropriate love.

I also felt my own mortality as we sat in the crematorium. With the next few months in my mind and all the potential risks I thought about my own funeral. What would I like? Here are the answers:

1) I'd like everyone to wear something to do with triathlon or dogs

2) I'd like to be cremated in my GB tri-suit with a Union Flag by my side

3) I'd like the Pharrell music 'Happy' to be played and if possible the Downs Syndrome YouTube clip shown too.

4) I'd like everything to be red, white and blue

5) I'd like donations to be for the kids at Larkrise to have a very special PE day at a very special venue.

6) I'd like it to be all about me!

And that's it really. Nothing particularly complicated. Basically I'd like a party and everyone is invited!

PART 8

As if the health system hasn't treated (or rather not treated!) me badly enough, the news I received this afternoon has absolutely floored me. Bearing in mind when the neurologist first contacted me I was told to stop driving immediately because I may have an epileptic fit and to stop exercising because I might die; today I received an email telling me that unless I stumped up

£245 for a private consultation, I will have to wait four-six weeks to see the same surgeon! Well actually the letter said 'he hoped to see me within four-six weeks', so actually it could be longer. And that's only for the consultation, not the start of treatment! How can that be? I just can't wait that long. I need to make progress. I need to start the race. I can't warm-up forever!

So I will borrow the money for the operation. Yes it's likely to be a stupid amount of money, but my mental health is priceless and I know I can't cope with a really long NHS wait. I want to be well by Christmas and training for Geneva in the New Year. I want to qualify for Chicago. I at least need to stand a chance.

On a positive note (yes there really is one!) I received a fabulous card from the girls I finished my football career with at Street Ladies Football Club. Such touching messages and photos I had never seen. They made me feel proud, happy and grateful that I spent time with them.

I also received a big bouquet of flowers from a boy's parents at school. They wanted to thank me for spotting his running ability and sign posting him… hopefully all the way to Rio!

Part 9

OK, so this race was never going to be a super-sprint, nor a sprint, perhaps not even a 70.3 but honestly a Deca-man?! Is that really necessary? Do I really need testing that much? Clearly I do because that's the race I'm in.

Somehow I've been entered into an event that I didn't know even existed! Sadly a slot in the ballot opened up and I lost!

Everything the neurologist told me was shit! His ego obviously got the better of him. Instead of simply saying I needed to speak to my surgeon he gave his opinion which was way out. Today I have all the facts, timescales, procedures, risks and potential outcomes. I paid Mr P £245 to tell me the real deal and as horrific as the information is, it is factually correct and I trust him. It was money well spent! In summary:

a) My operation costs £100,000+ and can't be done privately. It requires the best team in the best facility. He said I deserved it!

b) The operation will take up to 16 hours.

c) I will have to wait until Oct/Nov unless my clinical need changes – I pray it doesn't!

d) I will be in ICU/hospital for up to a month!

e) I will have a major wound ear to ear and across to my temple.

f) I will need 6-12 months off work

g) I will suffer emotionally

h) I can do some easy exercise – 3 x 40 minutes a week to keep me sane!

There it is in black and white! He told me to wipe a year

of my life away! So, how do you cope with a comment like that? I don't really know. It's so surreal. Our life has changed today, but actually it hasn't! It won't physically change for a few months yet. That's what Mr P says will be most difficult. Feeling pretty 'normal' now and yet knowing I will be an invalid in the future. Of course there is no choice, but I will walk into hospital feeling OK and will probably leave in a wheelchair.

I search for positives and find them. Mum will have had time to get better and will hopefully be strong enough to be there for me. I have the summer holidays to catch up with all my friends and family and have some fun. We can plan. The worry about funding an operation has gone. I know my aims for next year have been extinguished. I won't race in Geneva and I won't qualify for Chicago. But I can't just stop and say goodbye to 2015. Good things will still happen next year, they will just be different to what I thought a month ago.

I will document as much as possible and take lots of photos. I will create a story board, like Lance Armstrong, but my story won't be a lie. I will emerge stronger. Mr P said I may lose my 'competitive edge'. I'm not sure if he meant physically or mentally. I accept it will all take its toll physically and that the road to fitness will be long and tiring, but I can only see my desire to compete being greater. It's what makes me me – I hate losing. Don't get me wrong, I am a gracious loser. I do practise what I teach! I am a good sports woman, but I absolutely hate losing! I may end up technically being a 'completer' as opposed to a 'competitor' but I will be in a different race to everyone else. Every time I get into the pool/

lake (triathlon) or stand on the start line (running) I will already be in The Life's Winners' Race. I will be a cliché!

A friend had to put her dog, Charlie, to sleep today. I feel so sorry for her. It was a short illness (like my Charlie) and he didn't suffer. I will write a card and pop it through her letter box tomorrow.

I smashed my phone. Accidentally, but honestly could there be a worse time to be phone-less and to have potentially lost all my numbers? It's probably going to be expensive to replace, but as I said to Tim, money seems a little bit insignificant today, we still need it, but… hey!

My head is spinning and I feel quite poorly. It's probably just stress and tiredness, but I can't help worrying. Waiting is going to be difficult.

Part 10

It's exactly three weeks to the minute that my life, our lives changed. There are flowers in all rooms and the mantelpiece is filled with cards, but apart from that nothing's really changed. We are still going about our business as before – going to work, training a bit, baking cakes and going out with friends/family. But of course there is a difference. The countdown has begun and I am on 'the list'.

We talked about it all for the first time last night. Tim was upset about something pretty insignificant and this prompted the conversation. It wasn't emotional. It wasn't sentimental – we just talked about how we felt at that particular moment in time. Tim explained that his biggest fear was that I wouldn't be 'me' after the operation and he didn't know how I would cope with that. He said I was making things easier for him by being so positive and calm, but that he hadn't expected anything else.

I on the other hand have surprised myself. But on reflection I think I have subconsciously controlled my anxiety. Consider this: when Mr P told me the cold hard facts my stress level hit 100%. That level is unsustainable – for anyone. So I believe my subconscious quickly reduced it to minus 100%, so that as things get closer and more real I have different levels to move to. I think it will progressively build until the moment I am asleep and the operation begins. I think the first flash point will be when my car is sold and it leaves the driveway. Then things will start to become real. Things will actually start to change.

We are beginning to put some plans together for the summer holidays. David and Sandra are coming to stay. Roy and Sandra are camping nearby for a few days. I am going to Marsha's to help out at the London Triathlon. We are going to Poole to see Tim's mum for a mini-break. We are going to take the bikes to the Isle of White. I intend to see as many people as possible. I intend to create lots more happy memories that I can think about when I'm stuck in hospital or at home over the winter.

I flippantly posted on Facebook that I was raising money for Tooties through selling cakes! What I actually said was that I had lots and lots of bananas and was happy to make cakes for people if they could cover the cost of the extra ingredients with £3. 'After all', I wrote 'I need to start raising funds somehow'. It was joke, but people took me seriously and I have been baking ever since! I have explained but I think it helps people to feel they are helping me. And that's fine. I enjoy it and to be honest it does give me something to think about and do.

I've done my first turbo and run. Both were hot and both made me feel a bit woozy, but both helped me to relax and sleep better. Each day has to have a purpose. That's important. I've also got to keep a certain level of fitness for what's ahead. I can't turn into a burger-munching coach potato over night! After all, no-one ever wins a race by being lazy or badly prepared.

PART 11

We went out on Tim's new bike for the first time yesterday. I didn't feel great during it and I felt pretty rubbish after. This continued through the night and into today. Perhaps it's the heat, perhaps it's Tooties, perhaps it's just because I know? Everything makes me scared now. I try to trust Mr P and believe what he said – that I'm stable, but it's difficult when I have been told so many things that have been wrong. Perhaps I have to accept that I will feel poorly and have to slow right down. Exercise was supposed to lift me, but since I started again, I have felt worse. I will experiment with a few bits when I feel better, but I may have to accept that I need to stop.

I watched both the triathlons at the Commonwealth Games today. I took comfort from hearing about Helen Jenkins and Non Stanford. Helen was out for over two years, made a comeback and then missed the race today. And Non is out until 2015. If they can be positive and get back to their level then so can I. They both know it's a long road back and are prepared to start the journey. I suppose it's about finding the right map/sat-nav for you and following it. You have to trust it and not leave the planned route. It's easy to take a 'short cut' and end up in a traffic jam!

Talking of jam – I have been foraging today! I picked a carrier bag of wild plums. I will be making jam tomorrow!

PART 12

I had a dip at Vobster Quay today. My friend Susie was racing in a long swim (3.8km) and invited me over. I took my kit and did intend to join her for a 750m lap, but she was still a bit slow for me (judged by her first lap) and I felt too nervous to swim alone. I still didn't feel 100% and just didn't want to risk it. But after Susie finished she persuaded me to go in. I just did 10-15 minutes, but it felt lovely and it was nice to be part of it.

PART 14

I'm not writing a 'Part 13' – today has been a good day and doesn't deserve to be labelled with an unlucky number!

Today I felt much better. At times, back to my old self, so Dan, Murph and I went for a run along the canal. It wasn't as hot today and I wore a hat. The clamp on my head started when I finished but I drank two pints of water and it went. Perhaps that's the key: try to stay cool and drink plenty. It's been a good day.

Oh yes and I've spent nearly eight hours putting a photo album together. I searched through all my photos on my laptop and also scoured Facebook. If a photo exists it's in! I smiled a lot in that eight hours but also shed a few tears. It seemed 'funny' to see myself racing or smiling not knowing that Tooties was in my head. It was always there whatever I was doing and that's quite eerie.

PS. I cheated with the jam! I put gelatine leaves in because it wouldn't set and I didn't have the right equipment. It's a bit tart, but I don't mind that. I will give most of it away and if people don't like it…!

PART 15

The last few days have been pretty normal. I've paid attention to my hydration and have felt well. Not much 'clampy head' as we now call it. I've had a swim, a bike and a run. Obviously not hard, but I've still done it! And we went to see 'Singin' in the Rain' and had an 'all you can eat' buffet – as I said – pretty normal!

Then today I met Mum, June and Karen for coffee. Karen had a brain tumour 15 years ago. I had mixed emotions about seeing her. Part of me wanted to ask questions and hear her story, but part of me didn't. I still don't know how I feel following our chat. Every tumour is different. Every operation is different and we are very different. And as I keep reminding myself and everyone else – I don't have a choice. I have to face it!

I was contemplating this as I walked through the park on my way home. The darkness must have been written all over my face because a young Jamaican guy shouted out to me. He said, "You can smile you know!" This made me turn towards him and smile. He then said, "See I knew you could and now you feel better and the sun will keep shining down on you!" How lovely! And he was right – I did feel better!

PART 16

I had a really great four days in London with BFF Marsha and the RGActive gang. It was the London Triathlon weekend and we helped out on the RGActive trade stand. It was also our fourth anniversary! Marsha and I actually met at the 2010 race. I was walking around the exhibition stalls, proudly wearing my Budapest World Championship shirt. Marsha jumped out and introduced herself – she was going too! I didn't really think I would see her there, but hoped to. Then whilst waiting at passport control in Hungary I heard Marsha's voice! She still has a very distinctive American accent despite living here for 25 years! I tapped her on the shoulder and we spent the rest of the trip together! And that was that – BFFs!

Anyway back to this weekend – it was loooong and tiring but good fun. I still enjoyed watching others race, but I did have a pang of sadness when the faster ladies wave ran out of T2. They were running like I used to run and for the first time since Kitzbuhel, I missed it.

Someone upset Marsha. It was a very insensitive comment and Marsha felt very angry about it. She wanted to defend me. It wasn't said to me, but the story was re-told and although it was a tactless, thoughtless comment it didn't really bother me. However it did make me realise how much my condition affects others and that my loved ones desperately want to protect me. Marsha was asked what would happen if my operation went wrong?! I just told Marsha if it ever happens again, just say you don't know, but add that you do know what will happen if I don't have the operation – Rachel will go blind in one eye, she will have a stroke and she will die – that should shut them up!

PART 17

Team Abrams arrive this afternoon. I feel great today. The best day for ages. I had a really comfortable run with Murph and actually speeded up a bit because my heart rate stayed down.

As I ran I also thought about something people often say to me. They ask me if I question 'why me?' The answer is NO! I never have and I don't think I ever will. I don't feel sorry for myself. I have a great life. I have been successful in every way. I have a top career and am highly respected in my field. I have a loving family. My partner adores me. Materialistically I have everything I need. I have competed at the highest levels in amateur sports. I have wonderful friends. What more could I ask for? Of course I want my health back, but feeling sorry for myself just isn't in my recovery plan! It's simply a bad patch in an otherwise wonderful lifetime.

PART 18

Feeling great continued through our Team Abrams visit. We managed to laugh, fart, eat, ride, drink and swim all very successfully! It was a fab couple of days. However I am now learning that there is probably always going to be a trade-off and since they left I have felt like shit. I look terrible and feel terrible. My head hurts and I feel sick. I am trying to keep going though because I don't like wasting time. I will have plenty of 'down time', sitting around doing nothing in the near future – now I want to be as active as possible. But it's hard! I haven't even walked Little Big Murph yet although I have had my hair cut and advertised my car. Sad times.

I've just been to bed for a couple of hours. Clampy head has really got a grip! I must have slept for a bit, but then I started thinking, which as Tim says, is never a good thing! It's now pouring with rain and I am really wishing I walked Murph earlier!

So what was I thinking about? I actually felt quite cross with myself. I'm beginning to feel like I am giving in to feeling unwell and that going to bed in the afternoon confirms this. I feel quite miserable. Then I started thinking about being in hospital over Christmas or being too poorly to enjoy Christmas. So I have decided that if either scenario is likely I would like to celebrate ours early ie have Christmas Eve and Christmas Day before I go in. I'd like an 'open house' on Christmas Eve and then I'd like everyone to come to us for Christmas dinner. I'm even going to put the tree up!

My photo book is nearly finished. I've just got two pages left for this weekend with Roy and Sandra and my mum and dad's forty-fifth Wedding Anniversary – then the masterpiece will have been created!

Right better brave the elements now – Murph looks fed up!

Part 19

I'm pretty bored of being poorly now! More often than not 'clampy head' has a good grip. It makes me feel anxious and scared. I monitor every bit of me. I'm over analysing every physical change, but I just don't know what I'm supposed to feel. It seems like since I visited Mr P I have gone downhill – coincidence? Maybe, but when I felt OK waiting for my operation was bearable. Now it just worries me.

We did have a lovely weekend with family and when I am distracted I feel better. But when I am exercising I feel scared – what if I am putting myself at risk? I don't want to stop but maybe the gains are beginning to be out-weighed by the anxiety?! I'm sleeping really well and try to put a brave face on everything but I am beginning to feel worn down. It's not pain, it's a strange feeling. It's a pressure all over my head.

Part of me wants to keep up some level of activity because we are eating out such a lot! Our master plan of catching up with everyone is a lot of fun but it's also a lot of calories! Three Indians in six days is a bit much even for us! And in between that we have been out for another four meals!

Never mind – it's a once in a lifetime experience – I bloody well hope so!

My photo book entitled 'The Best Album Ever' is finally finished and has been ordered. I estimate a massive 30+ hours have been dedicated to this monster 100 page project. I thought I had finished it yesterday but then discovered the 'backgrounds' button. So this morning another two hours were spent choosing and adding different backdrops to every page! Honestly, it's probably a tad 'over the top' in places, but hey, it's mine and let's face it, when did I ever have/do anything like anyone else?! Xx

PART 20

Finally, I get to speak to Mr P. I think I could actually hear his eyes rolling in his head! He reassured me that it is 'normal' for me to feel worse now that I know the enormity of what I'm facing. He said that 'Tooties' will not have changed since the MRI scan and that I am safe. He was surprised my CT scan etc hadn't been scheduled and said he would sort it. He gave me the impression that everything was progressing as expected.

So I have tried to put my symptoms to one side and get on with my summer again. We went to the Isle of Wight for a couple of days and now I am staying in Poole with Murph at Nik and Gill's house (Tim is working). We had a great time – we did some cycling, some sea swimming and a fair bit of munching on lovely fresh food.

I am going to do the Poole Park Run tomorrow. I will obviously be sensible and keep my heart rate down. So 'what's the point in doing it?' I hear you cry! Well the answer is simple: I still don't think I will be last and even if I am I don't care. I just want to be around like-minded people who think about their personal well-being. Everyone will be doing their best whatever their level and whatever journey they are on. Murph will enjoy it too and I always like to see him smile!

On a completely different note, I have been very affected by the sad death of Robin Williams. I felt similar when Princess Diana died. The realisation that no matter how famous or rich you are, sometimes you just can't be saved. I think I feel particularly moved by Robin's suicide because we have just been through such a traumatic time with Mum. It made me wonder how close she has been? Perhaps it has never been an option for her? It would really hurt to think she did consider it. Not because I would judge her or think she had been selfish. Quite the contrary. I would just hate the thought that my mum had felt that desperate.

I understand some people have written some pretty harsh words about Robin. I don't think these people can have ever experienced real clinical depression up close. Don't get me wrong, Mum's illness has made me feel all sorts of things. I've felt helpless, frustrated and angry. At times I've felt uncontrollable rage and have taken it out on Tim or ran so hard it made me cry, but only because I couldn't help. It became about me and how I managed my feelings. And I have managed them. Over time I've found strategies that have helped me to cope and that's the difference I suppose. For whatever reason I've been able to find them, but sadly Mum can't and so her emotions spiral out of control. Even more sad is the fact that Robin Williams settled his battle with a rope. Terrible. Rest In Peace Robin Williams in the knowledge that you were loved and respected and will be remembered by me and many more, for all the right reasons. Xx

Part 21

So that's that done! My first event since being diagnosed. Murph and I finished the Poole Park Run in about 31 minutes. It's a very flat, fast course, which I have actually won in the past! I usually run 20 minutesish, so needless to say I'm not exactly celebrating my time! However what I did gain from today was an understanding of the mid pack. They are generally a different shape to the leaders, but apart from that everything is the same. Their heart rate monitors bleep, they check their watch regularly and they all 'blow out of their arses with effort!' They just move a bit slower! It's as serious back there. People still care. And that helped me to enjoy the race, because I still felt I was in one. Coming into the final 800m the pace did change (just as it does at the front) and in the last 100m people did sprint (just as they do at the front) and it did matter.

So despite my all time PW (to date – I obviously expect things to be much slower next year) – it was worth while and something I might look to do more regularly as I head towards the operation. It's a free way to be part of something I enjoy. Who knows, I may even meet and make new friends along the way?!

PART 22

I've left Tim in bed. We are still in Poole and I just couldn't sleep once I had sorted Murph's breakfast and let him out. My mind has now turned to school work and the amount I need to do. Of course some of it doesn't have to be done, but I want it to be done. I want to do it so that things tick along when I am off and I don't worry too much about it.

I'm also upset about something that's probably pretty trivial, but nevertheless, it's had an effect on me. I'm sorry this book is turning into a big moan! I thought it would be more amusing. I thought some of my experiences and situations would be funny. Hmmm? There has to be a funny side to this – doesn't there?

Part 23

OMG! Spooky situation coming up! So as you know we were away last week. Team Abrams kindly sent a 'thank you' card, which I obviously didn't see until I returned home. However in the meantime I bought a plaque to take into hospital with me. Can you imagine my surprise when I open my card and David/Sandra had written the exact same message inside?! Pretty special hey? It made me think two things: 1) that good friends clearly think the same as me and that's why they are good friends because they understand me and 2) I must emit positivity and I'm pretty happy about that!

The plaque and their message said 'Life isn't about waiting for the storm to pass, it's about learning how to dance in the rain!'

Then another friend popped round. He obviously asked how I was and I explained I was feeling good but that I sometimes feel a bit frustrated that I have to run so slowly, but that I pull myself together and remind myself that in a couple of months' time I won't even be able to get out of bed! Therefore, I should be grateful I am running at all! This prompted him to tell me about his last run. He wasn't enjoying it and felt tired and started to walk. Then I popped into his head and he thought 'poor Rachel won't be able to do this soon' and he started to run again. He felt motivated.

I'm glad I can do that. I hope that people will feel inspired by my thoughts and actions. An old friend once said to me, 'If there weren't any bad days there couldn't be any good days!' And he is right!

PART 24

I've been thinking about Tim a lot recently. I've realised that I probably haven't written as much as I should about him. He won't care because he's not really like that. He doesn't flourish on or need praise, but nevertheless, he does deserve it.

From Day 1 he has never wavered. I have seen the hurt and worry in his eyes. I have seen him weep a few tears and yet he stays strong for me. He does as much as he can to make my life easier. I think he probably always did – but now I notice it! And that's another positive to come out of this shit situation: I realise how much I love him and know how much he loves me. We are not married but we are joined. Tooties has brought us closer together. I think it has highlighted what is important – us. Tooties will go but we will still be together. Tim didn't need to say the vow 'in sickness and in health' to prove his commitment to me. He shows it every single day just by being here!

PART 25

OMG! I've got a sugar hangover! Tooties is changing me into a 'pudding eating machine!' We went to Za Za Bazaar last night, following a trip to the eye hospital (more on that later) and a visit to see 'Shrek the Musical'.

Now I usually demolish four plates of curry/Chinese and then pay a token gesture visit to the pudding section. I might put a few bits on my plate and have a taste of each item, but I have never actually eaten a whole bit of anything. Not until yesterday that is!

So I did my usual trick: first and second plates hardly touched the sides. Third and fourth plates satisfied me and I felt full. Visited the 'sweet bar' and picked out the six puddings I liked the look of. Not in a million years did I expect to eat more than half a dozen individual tasters. Fast forward a few minutes and I've done the lot! Yes – six puddings! And no, not just those little pots you sometimes get in those restaurants – six proper puddings! Here is a list: a bowl of rice pudding, a slice of carrot cake, a slice of chocolate torte, creme brulee, a piece of strawberry cheesecake and Mr Whippy ice-cream.

Yes, I did feel a bit sick, but I'm sure something in my head (probably that bloody Tooties) just kept pushing me on! "You can do it!" it whispered in my ear! Do what exactly? Oh yeah, feel sick and get fat at this rate!

When I finally woke up from my sugar-induced coma, I still felt sick and had a headache and ridiculously my skin felt sore to the touch! I swear I didn't eat a morsel until 1.30pm!

Anyway, back to the eye hospital. I spent 2.5hrs being assessed. As usual I didn't exhibit any classic problems or present the ones they would expect (I'm getting used to that!). However the outcome was encouraging. I was told that Tooties is pressing on the nerves which dilate my pupil and move my eye up and to the right. This means I have developed a blind spot to my right because my eye can't move far enough to actually see what's there and I have become short sighted because my pupil can't react and open when things are close to me. However she explained that if the operation goes to plan these problems should improve and may even restore themselves to normal. Obviously this is great news.

She did go on to warn me that things could get worse if the operation doesn't go smoothly, but I can't dwell on that. She also confused me a bit by saying that I didn't need to have the operation now and that in her opinion my symptoms didn't warrant it. She explained that because Tooties is slow growing, it may be years before my sight is permanently affected.

Really? Come on – would anyone really want to wait until everything gets worse before they actually do something about it? Apparently some folk do! She said some people prefer 'to wait and see'. Wait for what? Wait for the time bomb to go off and then panic! Not me! I don't care if I'm the healthiest, least symptomatic patient on the planet. I know Tooties is there and quite frankly, it's bloody well going ASAP!

I explained to her that it wasn't my sight that was really bothering me, it was the carotid artery thing which was stopping me training and racing and that that was making me feel disabled and changing my life.

I also think that the smaller it is the easier it must be to operate safely and remove it. It's beyond me why some people might wait. Each to their own I suppose, but as I've said before, this tumour picked the wrong triathlete to mess with. It's on borrowed time!

PART 26

A new Park Run PB post 'D-Day' (Diagnosis Day!) – 29.09 minutess 4th in AG. The results are coming back! And it was on a tougher course than last week. Murph and I ventured to Southwick Country Park for our inaugural local run. We jogged/walked there, steamed round with an average HR of 145bpm (whoopsie!) and then jogged/walked home. A glorious total of 7 miles.

Then in the evening a kind friend drove me to the Cotswold Water Park so that I could embark on a night swim. Let's just say, if he hadn't made an effort to take me I would have bottled it! Yes it looked fabulous, but it also looked very cold! And yes it was cold – bloody freezing actually! Ten of us braved it. We had to wear a glow stick on our wrist and another one was attached to the back of our goggles. The buoys were covered in Christmas lights! The course was 400m and I have to be honest, I didn't know if I was going to make a lap. I couldn't decide whether my senses were being deprived or over-loaded? It was silent, it was pitch black and everything was still. When I started to swim I could only hear my breathing and I could only see the glow stick on my wrist under the water. And it was cold, so cold. But it was strangely beautiful. I pondered on how surreal it was that I was swimming in the dark with a glow stick on my head, when in a few months I would be laid in bed with bandages on my head! I felt lucky to be experiencing something so different and tranquil. In reality I probably wouldn't have done this swim if I hadn't grown Tooties. I would have been worried about the late night or how it fitted in with my training. I would have missed out on something special.

I managed three laps. I felt obliged to do at least this since poor Nellend had stood patiently on the side and had given up his evening for my whim! But I was cold! I didn't ever warm up.

When I got home a 20min hot shower, a big bowl of porridge and a mug of hot chocolate sorted me out. Will I do it again – you bet!

PART 27

Today is supposed to be a full day of school work, but I've done about an hour. I just can't get my act together today. Perhaps I need to go for a run? I definitely need to go for a run! Mum is very low again.

PART 28

The situation with Mum got me down for a bit, but then I put it in a box in my head and refocused on the fact that I can't do any more than I am and that I need to think about my own health and find happiness and escapism where and when I can. So I travelled to Folkestone with Tim's security team to see what the 'secret art event' was all about. I figured I could run, swim and shop and finish the school holidays off positively, rather than just let them fizzle out. What a great decision! I loved it!

An artist buried 30 pieces of gold worth 10 grand in the harbour. I don't think any of 'us' treasure hunters really understood 'why?', we just wanted to find some! So I bought a spade and a hand fork and set to work. I spent over 11 hours digging. I only witnessed one find. A young lad found a piece after only 20 minutes of hunting in a place that had been covered many times before. What it showed was that anyone could find one, anywhere, at anytime. And I could relate to that, but on a very different level – on a philosophical level. The people on that beach were as likely to find a piece of gold as they were to find a tumour in their head. There was no pattern. The laws of probability kept changing as more/less people tried and as the tide came in or went out. It was random. And I liked that.

I also realised after about eight hours of digging that my mind was empty, it was a complete blank. By engrossing myself in the simple act of digging I had cleared my thoughts. I hadn't thought about Tooties at all and no-one else had reminded me either. I was the same as everyone else on that beach. We all had a common cause – we all wanted to find gold!

So did the artist achieve what he set out to achieve? Who knows? What I do know is that for 11 hours of my life I participated in a social experiment that brought out the best in people. I didn't hear a cross word. I didn't hear any swearing. Everyone was calm. Sometimes people said the odd word to the person in the next hole, but by and large, people just dug!

And I do have some souvenirs. I found four washers (decoys for the metal detectors!) which I have put on a piece of leather cord which was attached to my hand fork. I will wear them as a bracelet. I also have blisters and aching muscles! I feel like I did the day after my Ironman race. Every bit of me is sore, but it feels great!

Looking back it was pretty surreal. Hundreds of people moving sand from one place to another and then more people moving it back again! It was a free activity which everyone could participate in. An activity which will probably continue to occupy people for years to come. After all, less than 50% of the gold was actually found in the official event time, so there is plenty left!

Part 29

I realised last night that it really is my training that maintains my work-life balance. Because I wasn't rushing out of the door to do a session and Tim wasn't due home until 7pm, I found myself at school until nearly 6.30pm! I didn't have a reason to go home, so I found stuff to do. But the thing with teaching is the job is never finished. So now I see how people without other interests get sucked in or how people who don't focus on maintaining those interests finish up as 'just' teachers with nothing else in their lives.

I also thought about how kind people can be. I decided

that each week I would award cakes to a couple of people at school who have made my life easier or just a bit more pleasant. The two recipients were very touched today. One had gone over and above to sort an IT problem for me so that I didn't feel stressed and the other just asked quietly how my mum was and spent a few minutes chatting. So as I have already said and will continue to say, "It really is the little things that count."

PART 30

I think I was a little bit naughty today! You know, when you do that thing you have been told not to do just because you have been told not to do it?! Well I obviously know in my case that could be a tad dangerous, but I just had to take a 'controlled' risk. I pushed it a bit harder on the bike today. Not stupid hard, but harder than I have dared to since D-Day. I wasn't wearing my HR monitor so I don't really know how hard, I just know it felt a bit too hard!

Then I added a 15min jog, so in fact I did my first brick in nearly three months! Woohoo!

Why? I'll tell you why – because I have my CT scan tomorrow and if I'm honest I'm expecting the results to show that I should stop exercising completely. I know that makes what I did seem even scarier, but I'm just in that sort of mood! The date for my operation will be set soon and I'm ready. Well kind of…!

PART 31

CT scan done! That's it then. The team should be getting together and setting me a date.

PART 32

So I'm still running around trying to prepare for this elusive date which seems to be never coming. Work is full on, social life is full on, training /exercise regime is pretty much dormant! I've actually got a tyre – yes middle-age spread is spreading and let's just say it's not welcome. But what can I do? I can't train hard and I can't bring myself to diet. Our social life involves eating and drinking lots and it's fun! Plus the pressure in my head is pretty horrible at the moment and I don't feel like getting out there. After all, give myself a break, I'm poorly, I've got a bloody great golf-ball-sized lump in my head! And my mum is poorly. There are no laughs here! Or are there?

Yes there are, lots! We had a fab weekend with Marsha and John. I caught up with lots of RGActive friends, watched Marsha at the Big Cow and London Duathlon and laughed. Not at Marsha obviously, that would be rude!

PART 33

Today I feel flat, fat, poorly, tired, frustrated, sad, sick, fat, bloated, oh yes, did I mention fat? This has been a 'poorly' week. The weather has been pretty oppressive and my head seems to work like a barometer. As the air pressure climbs so does the pressure in my head and it's horrible. So for two days I could only just go to school – I couldn't manage any extra work or exercise. When the storm finally came I gave up and went to bed at 8pm, but unfortunately the air still hasn't cleared and I don't feel well.

I had a curry night with the Old Guard AVR girls last night. Of course I probably did eat and drink too much, but then there is nothing unusual in that! I woke up in the night with a terrible headache, in the usual place. It's very localised. I tried to persuade myself it would pass but it didn't, so I took some tablets. I was determined to get up early and run Little Big Murph round my 7.5 mile loop because we are off to Liverpool to see Juzzy and Big Phil and he will be in the van for a long time.

The alarm went off. I felt like shit. I got up, made a coffee, spilt the coffee and felt like shit. Put my HR monitor on – it has broken and I felt like shit. I started to jog. I knew instantly that my HR zoomed up. My head really hurt and my eye started to pulse – and yes I felt like shit. So after 200m I walked. After another 50m I started to cry. It was still dark and suddenly I felt very lonely. I also felt fat and stupid. There I was in my running gear feeling bloated, farting lots of curry farts, unable to move faster than a very slow snail. I felt ridiculous.

And now I'm home writing this I still feel all those things with an additional dose of frustration. If I knew I was just hungover I would grip myself by the throat and chuck myself back out the door and say, "Go run it off, if you suffer tough, it's self inflicted!" But because I don't know for sure and because I have had a very bad headache in the night I have to be cautious. And that's what it is. Writing this down has made it make sense. I am feeling like this but I have had to accept I'm poorly. Most of the time my life carries on as normal, but occasionally, like this morning, I am reminded. I have to be careful. And I hate it!

PART 34

It's been a looooooong time since I visited this book! I'd love to say it's because I have been having such fun I haven't had time, but sadly not! It's not all been bad I hasten to say, but some of it hasn't been much fun!

Of course as expected Liverpool was great and we really enjoyed spending time with muckers Big Phil and Juzzy. They are having a tough time at the moment and it was nice to be able to repay some of their thoughtfulness with a bit of our support. And naturally we laughed a lot!

Then the storm began. Mum went back into hospital, my triathlete friend Susie went into ICU, Tim was away a lot and I picked up a cold. I managed to ride backwards and forwards to the hospital to see Mum, but basically once she went home I crashed and burnt spectacularly! I came home from school at 11.45am and by 12.15pm I was fast asleep until 5pm! But it did the trick and an early night with another 11 hours sleep and I felt ready to 'dance in the rain' again!

A week on and I am waiting by the door mat to see if my London Marathon ballot application has been successful or not. Tim is a reject, but I have a hopeful feeling! Of course if I am lucky I will defer it until 2016. My cousin Mike got in, so it could be a family affair! That would be really nice. More marathon memories for Mum. She always really enjoyed those trips.

Part 36

I am a reject! The dreaded 'sorry' magazine plopped onto the door mat with a sad thud! Oh well! Linzi was rejected too, so we have pledged to enter again next year. If we are still unsuccessful in the ballot we will go down the charity route. So in 2016 my family will be running the London Marathon!

Lots of strange dreams/nightmares at the moment. Very disturbing. Interrupted sleep doesn't suit me!

Part 37

I suppose it's to be expected. My book entries have dwindled! It's not because I can't be bothered, it's because everything has been pretty much the same. I would just be banging on about the same things! Pretty dull for you, the reader!

Every day people ask me how I am and whether I've got a date yet? I reply positively to the former and negatively to the latter. The enquirer responds with disgust and disbelief in an 'I'm supporting you' kind-of-way. Now I'm not complaining that people are interested, I'm just amazed! I'm so bored of waiting and being asked that I assume everyone else must be too!

So imagine the responses when I now say, "It's been delayed until Christmas/January time." The ranting begins! "Why? That's ridiculous…"

PART 38

OMG he let it slip! The registrar I spoke to today about my nightmares (amongst other things) told me my operation is scheduled for December! He didn't give me an exact date, but he did say more than Mr P's secretary would. She treats everything like it's a national security risk!

I have mixed feelings. Excitement on the one hand – the waiting is nearly over. Fear on the other hand – the waiting is nearly over! Yes I want it to happen. I know it has to happen, but gulp, I'm scared – it's going to happen! There are still so many unanswered questions. I am worried about how much pain I am going to endure and how long I will be incapacitated. My friend Susie was in ICU for 10 days recently and she looked awful. I was shocked. I know I am going to look worse. I just want to be 'me' again. Of course everything is still the same, more or less, but it isn't really! I have a tumour in my head. I know it's there. Everyone knows it's there. I can do everything I used to do but not in the way I want to do it. I want to run as fast as I can. When will that be? How will Mr P know when it's safe? God I miss racing!

Part 39

Oh good, the nightmares have stopped. Great I can get to sleep easily. Bugger, I'm waking up at 5am, wide awake with butterflies in my tummy!

I'm writing my Will today.

Part 40

Writing my Will was a very positive experience for lots of reasons. I enjoyed it in a bizarre way! I didn't see it as a sad thing or as something depressing. I saw it as a celebration of those I love. It made me think about who is important to me and why. For the first time in my life I realised I was thinking about giving without ever being thanked.

It was liberating. I wrote it for today, hoping that it won't be read for many, many years. I also wrote a poem to go with it. I am including it here because when I survive and this book is read or even published, I want people to know that even when the chips were down I was still me. I think the poem smacks of me – I hope it does!

If Tooties Wins.

If I die through this process,
Please don't just cry,
Weep and wail and scream "why?"

As you know,
I wasn't ready to go.
There were lots more races to win
And places I hadn't been!

Of course you loved me, adored me, respected me, blah
blah blahed me
But let's be honest, no-one loved me more than I loved
me!

So there it is, Tooties' won
But throughout it all I had some fun
So many memories, so many friends
That's what makes it such a bearable end
A small but perfectly formed family unit
I know they are proud to have had me in it.

Please always miss me, commemorate me and remember
me
Whenever you see a runner whizz by or a cyclist fly by
Look up and say "hi"
I know I will be there – after all, I was a winner not a
sinner!

So there it is in just a few lines,
The reason why I was a PE teacher and not a poet of
the time

I was a gift from God
A pleasure to know
And boy oh boy did my head often grow!

So smile a smile and laugh a laugh
The race was raced, I wore the vest
And do you know what?
I really did always do my best!

You see the reason I feel blessed and enjoyed writing my Will was because so many people are in it! The solicitor said that she had fun writing it with me and that she had never written one quite like it! I took this as a big compliment.

There was also a comedy moment when she suggested I had a critical illness and I replied, "Oh I'm not poorly enough to have one of those!" She actually laughed at me. Perhaps I am still in denial. I think I probably am. It's difficult to think about what my prognosis is without an operation, when I feel pretty well most of the time! If I hadn't seen the scans I could probably convince myself there was nothing wrong and I was just attention seeking!

Part 41

This has probably been my best ever birthday. I had a fab fortieth, but overall I think this one has topped it. Talk about being spoilt. And I don't just mean presents. Yes, I have had lots and lots of money spent on me but the best bits have involved Tim and my F and Fs. A weekend in London with Marsha, John, Juzzy and Big Phil. A mini-break with Tim and Little Big Murph on the Isle of Wight and a tea party with fireworks on my actual birthday. Not to mention pizza with my school buddies and a trip to see the West End show 'White Christmas'.

Of course there also had to be some moments of madness! We actually photographed a ghost, had an 'altercation' with two pensioners and I managed to fire a rocket across the garden, missing my F and Fs by inches! Like Tim said, there was always going to be an incident with me involved!

I wonder what it's like to be boring or predictable?

PART 42

Breakdown time. I started to cry tonight. Tim asked the obvious question "why?" and I honestly didn't know. I just wanted to cry! When I did try to verbalise my feelings they didn't really make much sense. Basically to cut a long story short, I felt exhausted. Worn out by the wait. Fed up of having my life on hold. Sick of being, asked "have you got a date yet?"

PART 43

I've got it! A date! Of course, it's not an absolute certainty but it's as confirmed as these things can be. After last night's melt down I decided to try and take some control back, so I called the hospital again. The secretary tried to fob me off again but when I cornered her and told her that I knew she knew because the registrar had let December slip she caved in! "Naughty registrar," she said! So she reluctantly unveiled the date – MONDAY 15TH DECEMBER 2014.

PART 44

The plans have begun. I will finish school on the 5th Dec. This will give me a few days to reset and prepare. Not that there is much to do. My PJs have been packed for months! Tim and I discussed it and we decided that I needed a rest. Time to reflect and slow down. So I've booked a family Christmas dinner, a shopping trip, various coffees/meals with friends, a Santa 5KM run, lots of 'training' – it's going to be soooo restful! I'm still looking at everything in the same way. Make the most of every day. There will be plenty of time to sit on the sofa and watch TV when I have to!

PART 45

I had an interview today to be a Specialist Leader in Education (SLE). It's basically an advisory role in the Trowbridge area. The panel were fully aware of my health issues and reassured me that this wasn't an issue. If successful, they are perfectly happy to delay my training and start date. I felt very proud to have been invited to apply and very valued. My career has been validated and my ambition may be realised. World, I mean local domination, I mean awareness of SEN PE!

PART 45

Two weeks today I finish work. The time is flying by, largely because I am still so busy. Just as I start to see the end of my 'to do list', more things get added.

My friend Lynne commented on this. She was concerned that I'm not being kind enough to myself and that my work is acting as scaffolding, holding me together! And she is probably right, but that's how it has to be. When I walk out of the building on 5th Dec, I need to feel relaxed about how I have left everything. I know I can't think/do everything, but I can leave it as healthy and structured as possible. That way I will feel happy, the sports coaches will feel supported and the kids will not suffer.

I can feel my anxiety building, but I can also feel everyone's support lifting me. The staff and kids have already begun wishing me well and telling me I will be missed. I know I'm going to cry at some point. I will probably sob. I am not a workaholic. I have always put myself, training and family first but God I'm going to miss them! The kids and friends – I'm so lucky!

PART 46

We had a very productive weekend at The Running Show. Tim was exhibiting. We were raising the profile of next year's events. It was a great networking opportunity for me as it turned out! I met someone who was interested in putting an entry from this book into his magazine! I also chatted to the show organiser who was interested in me doing a motivational seminar at next year's show and publicising this book! Good hey, well it's exciting to feel people are at least interested.

Part 47

I cried at school today. One of my sixth form students made me a beautiful card. He was so pleased to give it to me and insisted I opened it there and then. Whoosh I was off! Not because it made me sad. Not even because stuff is becoming more and more real. I cried because I realised I really had had an impact on his life! He had thought about me. He cared enough to spend his own time designing this card. Amazing! That's why I do it. That's why I try my best every day. I'm not saying I am 'Wonder Teacher'. I have 'off days'. Days when I drag myself through lessons, but I never forget that these kids deserve my attention. They deserve the best I can be!

Part 48

"So why do you have to have an operation on your head?" asked a student.
"Because my brain is so big they need to take some of it away!" I replied.
"Is that because you are so popular?" she quizzed. "Because you are popular you know, we are all going to miss you."

And this comes from a young lady who has severe

learning difficulties. I'd argue she has more emotional intelligence than many of us! Not wanting to worry her I responded with, "Thank you for saying that, but being popular doesn't make you poorly, it just means lovely people like you say lovely things to people who need to hear them!" She grinned and we continued with the lesson.

Sometimes I think their world must be a beautiful place to live. It is simple. They say what they think and believe what they are told. They trust. They forgive. They love in a very pure, innocent way. Beautiful x

PART 49

I've had a quick flick through this book to date and I have realised that my ramblings were much longer in the beginning. I don't know why? Perhaps my feelings were more heightened six months ago? I was 'excited' about entering the race! Perhaps I've just adapted to having Tooties and the 'training' is beginning to plateau?

What I do know is that in training terms I have prepared for this race the best I can. I have focused. I have considered every aspect. I have controlled the controllables and considered the things I can't control. Now I need to taper! With two weeks to go I need to rest and stay healthy.

I am still fit. In relation to 99% of 40-something ladies in the UK, perhaps even the world, I am fit! I can still swim 2km, run 10km and bike for 2hrs without being exhausted. I am still working full-time, socialising full-time and living full-time! I am fit both physically and mentally. My support team have looked after me and kept me going. I am ready now. I just need to rest, absorb the training, concentrate on the finer details and be ready to hit it hard when the claxon goes!

PART 50

It's one minute past midnight and I can't sleep. I've just realised what a difficult day I've had! Work was busy, then I had my pre-op stuff done, then my journey to the train station was stressful, then I received my Will via email and then work stuff got busy again! You see I'm still trying to balance everything, still trying to be fair, still trying to consider everyone else's feelings. But do you know what – I'm on the edge, and it's not of Lady Gaga's 'Glory!' It's been a horrible day in reality and yet I've still put a jokey post on Facebook and had a laugh at dinner with a couple of friends. I've hidden it today. Today was a 'stiff upper lip' day. Today I have felt scared and sad. I nearly wrote another late night FB message expressing this, but I didn't. I'm always a bit dismissive of others who 'attention seek' in this way: it's not my style, so I'm writing this instead. This is what happened today: school began with the usual bus dramas, but they were sorted and my trip went ahead. The kids were a credit to themselves and it was a big success. Tim was away working, so Mum and Dad agreed to take me to Bristol for my pre-op assessments. Whilst we were waiting they asked if they could accompany me. I agreed so long as Mum was strong enough to cope – she knew what I meant. I warned them I had lots of questions and that some stuff would be difficult for them to hear. They still came in. And it was pretty horrific. I'm really tired now so this can wait. Night night x

Part 51

Sorry about that abrupt finish. I suddenly closed down. But it's OK now. It's a great feeling when a day that starts badly suddenly saves itself! You think the doom is going to continue and then whoosh, it's a great day! I didn't sleep. I felt anxious and upset all night, but then as soon as I got to school my friends and pupils lifted me back up. I felt loved and re-energised.

I was reading an article on the internet entitled 'A letter to a friend with a brain tumour'. It was aimed at people like me and was very insightful. He started by saying he would tell me the real story and not what 'the medical professionals' will tell me! That was very interesting, but for me, the most insightful part was about finding clarity in your life. I totally agree with him and this is why I actually found myself saying to someone "If I had one wish it wouldn't be that Tooties had never existed!" Now that might seem a bold, even absurd statement, but it's true. I am 44 years old and have a gift – clarity and perspective. I know exactly who and what are important to me. Not many people are lucky enough to reach this point at such a relatively young age. He said to enjoy this period because it is pure and honest, and sadly for him, it didn't last. I pray with all my heart that I can hang on to it, because honestly, the last six months have been some of the best times of my life!

Three people have said, "You are very brave" to me today. I am grateful for their kind words but I do want to put this out there: I am not brave, I am just coping as best I can. Brave people take risks to make something better. I am not taking a risk. I am doing what I have to do, there really is a difference. I smile and make jokes because that makes me and those around me feel better. We are coping and that means we are winning and everyone knows I hate losing!

PART 52

There are now just two days to go until I walk out of school knowing that the next time I see the kids it will all be over and Tooties will be gone. I have started to receive flowers and cards and my nerves are building. My sleep is all over the place and worry dreams about PE are slipping in.

I am nervous. My pre-op info has scared me. It warns that 1-1000 people experience 'awareness' during their operation which basically means they wake up because the levels of anaesthetic are too low! That's not a good statistic! In my tumour-filled mind it makes it quite likely! That really frightens me. The info says let your doctor know as soon as possible if this happens to help them learn and help future patients! Sod that! Just bloody keep me asleep!

My other worry is that 'this' might be as good as it gets and that I'm being unrealistic and selfish to push for more. Lots of patients settle for what I have. They just wait it out and enjoy their lives as they are. But I want what I had and that puts me into conflict with myself. One side says, "This life is pretty good. Everything is really quite normal. You can still swim, bike, run and work. Nothing has really changed, you just can't race." Then the other side jumps in, "But that's not good enough. You are a competitor. You need challenge and effort and progress. You need to race. You need to feel that 'sweet spot' again to feel like you!" And that's it in a nutshell really, what if I can't? What if it goes wrong? What if it goes well and I just can't regain it? These thoughts are probably very normal, but they are keeping me awake. And now that I am awake I feel in a constant state of anxiety. It's incomprehensible to fast forward two weeks and picture myself in Intensive Care. I just can't process it. How can that be me?

PART 53

I have finished – school has finished – what a finish! I've had a lovely week. Flowers and cards and gifts have flooded in. Our house is like Inter-Flora! A few people cried as they hugged me, but I managed not to. Even when the Head called me to the front in assembly and everyone clapped. I felt strong and energized. But when I got home I completely crashed and burned. Every bit of me ached. It was just like the 'post-race' lethargy I get after a really hard event. I could hardly get out of the chair!

Part 54

I had my first operation dream. It wasn't a nightmare but it was unpleasant and it was enough to wake me up and get me up! I was laid in a very narrow bed with my head all bandaged and I had an excruciating pain in my right ear. They didn't know what was causing it, so I got up and had a look around! There were kids running around making lots of noise and I asked if they could go away because I was feeling a bit poorly!

Part 55

So as all athletes and performers know, the week before the big event can be very up and down. You start to focus on all the minute details. In fact you probably start to obsess about all the minute details! You play the race over and over in your mind. You hang onto the saying 'piss poor planning makes a piss poor performance!' So you plan a bit more! That's exactly how I approached this week. I finished school with a week to go so that we could have some 'down' time, but also have some fun. I put a timetable together ensuring we saw as many people as possible. I bought a beautiful dress and shoes for my BIG Christmas party. We planned shaving my head as an accessory! I entered a Santa dash the morning of my hospital admittance and even thought about what I would eat! I was going to put two bags together. My ICU bag and my 'I'm getting better' in hospital bag. I wanted to show Little Big Murph and Tim how much I loved them by cuddling up on the sofa and going for long runs (I think Tim would prefer the cuddles, LBM would grab both!).

And the plan began well. I finished school on a high, with lots of cards and flowers and love. I didn't even cry! I left feeling like it had been the perfect send off and I felt relaxed as I walked out the door. The plan pretty much started to pixelate as soon as I got home!

Richard called to tell me Mum had relapsed again and that she was in a bad way. Coming to the tests with me clearly hadn't helped, but she had been losing control for a while. They had decided not to tell me because they wanted me to enjoy my week – it was the right decision and I was grateful for it. Realistically it was naive of us to think that my situation could give Mum strength. It was always going to go badly wrong. I realise that now. Her only daughter has a brain tumour!

Then our fun began. We went shopping to Gun Quays in Portsmouth. As usual I spent waaaayyyy too much but it was a good day out. Then the week really unravelled. Mr P's secretary called to say my operation was being postponed until January because another lady had a higher clinical need and not all my tests had been done. We were speechless, then angry. Everything had been planned to the nth degree and now they were changing it, just like that! They gave me some test times for the next few days and wished me a Happy Christmas. So we rallied ourselves and began re-planning the next few weeks. What should I do about school? I couldn't face going back if my op was in January, but then again I didn't want to use some of my six months full pay unnecessarily. We decided to wait until after my tests to see what my SMT thought was best. We needed time to readjust.

Oh well, at least I was finally having my tests done. The race had been postponed, not cancelled. How could I possibly know as I laid on the radiographer's bed, that what was supposed to be a routine procedure would once again change the course of our lives? Only I could do that! The dilator drug was put into my body. It was supposed to open up all the blood vessels in my head so that Mr P could see which vessels he could shut off during the op if I had a stroke. Oh if only it was that simple! Suddenly I could feel this horrible pressure in my head, but more frightening was my HR and BR - they started to climb – 50% higher than normal! I could feel it all happening. Tim called the nurse – then it was Code Blue! I don't remember much, just people asking questions and getting on my nerves! They put me in the scanner (so I didn't have to go through it all again another day) and I fell asleep. When I woke up I panicked a bit. I couldn't get my balance and I felt really woozy. I also peed so much the bed pan overflowed! I was taken to the recovery area for observation, then admitted to a ward and then told I needed to stay overnight. Imagine my horror – no PJs! I was pretty tired so I slept well and woke up thinking I would be going home. When Tim arrived he actually thought I would be sat in the lobby waiting to go home! But my vision had changed. I nearly didn't tell anyone. I thought "If I do they will probably change my date again and everyone has been messed around enough!" I also thought Mum could do with the extra time, perhaps she could rally. But a nagging voice (probably God) told me not to be so stupid. My health should come first, so I told them. I was sent for an eye test and then the real action began! X

PART 56

I didn't need a test to show me I couldn't see much with my right eye, but what did shock me was when the nurse asked me to tell her the letters on the board, I couldn't even see the board! Last week during my pre-op tests I could see at least two lines of letters. In fact I couldn't even see where she was pointing and I only knew she was there because she was moving! And then it happened, both Mr P and his registrar came out into the corridor to see us. They didn't even take us aside. Mr P simply said, "This is not good, you now have a higher clinical need than the lady who pushed you down the list. You will now have your op Monday as originally planned and I'd like you to stay until then." Bloody hell – still no PJs! Once again I went into a pretty irrational thought mode: the spare bedroom isn't ready for Big Gill, my clean clothes haven't been put away, I didn't clean my bikes and pack them away, I didn't appreciate my last run with Murph enough, I hadn't even given Murph a proper kiss and cuddle when we left. For God's sake it was supposed to be a two hour test! I was supposed to be home for lunch! All that minute detailed planning evaporated. I wouldn't be dancing in my new dress and shoes at the school Christmas party and I wouldn't be dashing around like a Santa. I wouldn't even be eating my favourite tea! Being a control freak is tough don't you know! X

Part 57

Great news, I am allowed to go home for a few hours tomorrow which by the time we drive there and back pretty much means I am on day release! I need to tidy up a few loose ends around the house, give LBM a BIG cuddle and a nice walk and spend a bit of 'real time' with Tim. It's going to be action packed but I am excited that I have some control over the day and can spend some quality precious time with everything important to me. We are going to have a nice lunch and try to relax. It's been mad. Even tonight whilst I have been lounging about, Tim has been off driving for the school Christmas party.

I can't sleep – it's a 'roid thing! I'm fully awake and hungry. That's probably why one of the common side effects is weight gain – you're up all night with the munchies! They took me for another CT scan with contrast at 11.30pm which obviously hasn't helped. It was a bit of a shock when two porters arrived. I was just enjoying a very good, inspirational, cheesy film called 'If I Could Fly?' and they dragged me and my bed away! But I'm ok. I've written an email to Mum for Richard to read and then give to her on Sunday. I know I will be seeing her tomorrow for a few minutes on my way back to hospital, but I just wanted her to know how I feel and to be able to see how I feel whenever she is up to it. I have pretty much done a full circle with how I feel about

Mum's illness. My feelings for her have never wavered but boy have I been angry, bitter, frustrated etc about the depression. It's definitely the illness I loathe and not Mum. I think I fully understand it now. Her depression consumes her. She is so devastated, feels so guilty and yet so disabled she just can't move from her bed. I don't have any expectations now. I'd just like her to be well enough to enjoy life again and to share some more good times with my dad.

Two days to go now until the hooter sounds. I will begin carbo-loading tomorrow. I'm looking at it like a deca-man. I've got to get the calories in even if I don't really feel like it, but then I can't remember the last time I stopped eating so it shouldn't be a problem!

PART 58

What a fun, fabulous day I have had. Tim and Nik picked me up around 11am and we headed back to Trowvegas. I spent an hour or so tidying and sorting a few bits. You know the sort of things that would bother me if I didn't! Then Big Gill arrived and we took Murph and Flo Flo for lunch. And very nice it was too! I had a delicious pudding – well I am carbo-loading don't you know!! Then we went back home and cut my hair. It took ages because it is so thick. It's not my best look, but it's not too shocking. This chick can rock most looks!

Next destination, Mum and Dad's. They didn't know I was coming, so the looks on their faces will stay with me forever. When Dad opened the door he looked confused, then worried and then over-joyed once he realised everything was still ok. He squeezed me so long and so hard I couldn't breathe! Richard was there (I wasn't expecting him to be there until Sunday) and explained they were waiting for a doctor. Mum was at her worst. She had taken a fall in the night. And she looked dreadful – two black eyes and a swollen forehead – definitely worse than I expected. I whispered, "Mum it's me. I've come to see you." Mum opened her eyes. She really couldn't process what was happening for a few seconds and then she grabbed me sobbing, "It's my baby girl!" Priceless. Those were some of the best minutes in my life so far. I will never forget them. I was able to give her what she needed and I felt at peace. She just wanted to hold onto me, her baby girl. And that was enough. I knew I could go down to theatre on Monday without holding her hand. I will have Tim and he is enough – more than enough. Mum and Dad will be with me in my heart and I know that. It's funny how calm I felt. I didn't cry. I wasn't hiding anything. I didn't want to cry. I felt happy. And then I left. Tim had waited outside. We talked briefly about what happened and then it was done. Time to go back to begin the last phase. Time to settle back down, put my feet up and rest.

Part 59

Yes the sleeping pill worked. It gave me six wonderful, dreamless hours of quality sleep. I did wake up around 4.30am, feeling a bit anxious about the 'event' but managed to doze until the ward officially woke up. Then I had an athlete's breakfast of porridge and toast, had a nice shower with my super expensive but totally gorgeous 'poorly smellies' and settled down on the iPad 4!

The registrar visited. I was looking my best and I think he liked my new hair-do. At least he recognised me! After my eye tests on Thursday, literally 40 minutes after meeting me he didn't! How rude, he obviously didn't know who he would be cutting up, he does now!

He went through everything. He even drew me a picture. And I finally understand what has been happening to me and why the dilation drug did what it did. And I feel better. I know what his race plan is. I know what the race will look like on a) a bad day – not my course – pretty difficult to cope with this result when I've trained and prepared for so long and so well; b) an OK day – result acceptable but I had to work bloody hard for it; and c) the perfect day – when I am in the zone and it feels great. I know I'm racing at my best, reaching my potential, getting the outcome I deserve!

Of course there are risks, big risks, but they are calculated, as safe as they can be risks. Just leaving Tooties there will be a catastrophic risk. There isn't a choice. I've even thought about the nicknames and jokes I will make about myself if they have a bad race. It will be fine. As long as I can still be me and laugh at myself then the world will be a good place.

The surprise footnote was that I am having a BOGOF op! They are going to take Tiny Tooties out at the same time! With a slight diversion they can grab that little bastard too – good news!

So that's about it for today really. Tim et al are expected very soon. My phone and Facebook have been going mental and once again I feel loved. The registrar said I am one of the most positive patients he has ever met. He was very flattered when I said he would get a mention in my book. In fact if they execute their perfect race I will dedicate the whole bloody book to them! Actually it will say: For Tim, Mum and Dad, Mr P, Mr Italian Man and all the people who have laughed and cried with me and at me along the way!

Part 60

Well here we are. The final countdown has really begun. Can you hear the 'Rocky' music in the background? I'm waiting for my sleeping pill. I am feeling a mixture of excitement and fear, but also a calmness. I feel strangely euphoric. I have caught and wrapped so many Facebook/text/phone/FaceTime/Skype hugs around me I am practically falling over with the weight of support. Tim and I talked about outcomes and the future. Neither of us is an idealist. Neither of us feels like life hands us things easily, but we both agree we are tight. We are a unit. We are a team that can face challenges and overcome them. We are not scared by the future. We are excited. I was told today that I have only been receiving 66% of the amount of blood to my brain that I should. It explains a lot about my immune system and health. It shows how efficient my CV system is. But above all, dear competitors, it shows me that you have had it easy! So watch out in 2016-2017 cos I will be back and I will be fully functional. You haven't even seen me leave second gear!

I found this poem:

If I should go tomorrow
It would never be goodbye,
For I have left my heart with you,
So don't you ever cry.
The love that's deep within me,
Shall reach you from the stars,
You'll feel it from the heavens,
And it will heal the scars

Anon

Part 61

This part is being written retrospectively – operation plus five days. I slept well and felt pretty relaxed. Tim arrived at about 7am and then the porters collected me at 8am. We were taken to the pre-theatre area and met with the anaesthetist and Mr P. I merrily showed my photo book to anyone who stood still for too long – not realising that my enthusiasm was actually making the team nervous! At 8.30am the actual procedure hadn't been finalised. My new developments had thrown extra issues into the pot and the risks and outcomes suddenly became very different and very frightening. We were looking at physical paralysis and a complete loss of eye function including the ability to lift my eye lid. The reality unfolded – the tumour would not be completely removed. I would need either another operation or radiotherapy. I may even need a carotid artery reconstruction using a vein from my leg! What became very clear was that we were only in the first stage of a multi-stage approach. I've had better starts to a week!

Tim was asked to leave and I was taken into the anaesthetist's area. I felt very calm. I really wasn't scared. When he asked me if I had anything to say I simply replied, "Thank you for looking after me and doing your best." He said no-one had ever said that to him before. And so I thanked God. I thanked Him for giving me enough strength and gratitude to recognise this man and make him feel appreciated. I had enough peace and love in my heart to share it and that made me feel happy. I didn't fight the drug. I just let myself go.

12 HOURS LATER

I woke up in ICU. They ask lots of questions and ask you to do lots of physical stuff to assess function. Tim arrived and I gave him a big bogey! That's what I did. I couldn't breathe so I picked a monster and handed it to him. I really wanted to flick it but he said I wasn't allowed! I was in a lot of pain and then I started to be sick. Apparently it smelt and looked foul. I just knew it hurt and that it frightened me. My whole body screamed with pain. In particular the creases in my elbows hurt – Tim massaged me gently and I felt better. The next 24 hours passed in a haze of thirst, assessments and pain. I couldn't get comfortable. I wasn't confused. I knew that Big Gill and Nik were there with Tim. But the monotony of pain is actually boring! Lying in that much pain is frustrating. I now understand why people with chronic pain conditions end it all. I asked when I would feel better and they just reassured me I was in the worst phase and it would be over in a few days. And it was!

Part 62

It's all very confusing. I have very mixed emotions. The operation was successful but the outcomes and plans are not yet known. It will be months probably. I can move properly though and I'm alive, but I can't see out of or open my right eye. I moved from ICU to the high dependency area in record time (24hrs) and have just been told I will move to my own independent room tomorrow morning. Apparently my physical progress is remarkable, but that doesn't have any link to the outcomes or next stages. Basically my fitness pushed me beyond the compromise of the tumour. I outperformed my illness. My fitness then took me through a very difficult 12 hour scalp and rummage. It then lifted me through the initial stages at an incredible rate. But I'm scared of it now! I'm scared that people will expect too much and try to push me on too quickly. I want to create a stable platform. This base has to be solid before we move on. I won't be rushed. I'm staying here until I feel confident that I know and understand what is happening to me and what my options/outcomes are. Just because it is Christmas week I am not putting the 'head thing' on hold! But for now I feel good. I feel better physically than I thought I would at this stage. All my tubes are out (head drain, arterial canular, chest canular, three arm canulars and a catheter) I can walk a few metres, eat soft food, smile and enjoy all my visitors. I'm back on Facebook and appreciating all the kind messages of love and support. One post had nearly 4000 hits – wonderful! I've even had a Skype chat with a triathlete friend in New Zealand.

Any worries? Well I'm not a machine so obviously yes, but they don't dominate or consume me. I give them a bit of time. A measured respect, but as I sit here writing, allowing myself to dwell on 'what ifs?' will only achieve one thing. It will stop me sleeping! Hmmmm? Doesn't take a brain surgeon to tell me that's a stupid thing to do then! It's Day 6. I need to be thankful for feeling bright and progressing well. I need to rest and clear my mind. I don't even have any concrete facts to worry about or consider, so it really is a waste of my time and energy. So for now, I am just going to snuggle down and look forwards to tomorrow and my new en-suite facilities! Night night. Xx

PART 63

I haven't mentioned that as I laid on the operating table, Mum was admitted to the RUH. Obviously not having her with me has been tough, but I feel comforted knowing that she is being cared for properly. We have spoken on the phone and I have reassured her that I am ok. Of course it's a very stressful time for Dad. He is travelling from one hospital to another every day, but I am sure he feels better knowing we are both safe. Richard is staying with him, so he doesn't have to worry about driving or what he is going to have for his tea!

PART 64

It's Christmas Sunday and earlier this morning I asked if I could go to the hospital chapel. A lady came to collect me and pushed me in a wheelchair, bearing in mind I still have a catheter. The bag has been removed because I am retraining my bladder, so the tube has a valve on the end, which I can open when I feel the need to 'go'. The chapel was full of old people. I was the youngest by at least 20 years! Anyway, somehow during the service I managed to knock my valve and so as my carer wheeled me away, I left a big puddle! I could have ignored it, but no! I decide to shout back into the room "Whoops, look who weed in church, Happy Christmas!" I'm sure God raised his eyebrows and thought "trust her!"

PART 65

Whoops I've had another comedy mishap! I wasn't allowed to have my catheter removed until I had emptied my bowels. The problem was I hadn't been able to open mine. My pain management drugs had been well and truly blocking me up! Actually I hadn't been for ten days! Obviously drastic action was needed. Dyno-rod were busy so suppositories were used! I asked if I could go on a proper toilet. I knew that ten days' worth was never going to fit in a bed pan!

But it was my first time out of bed since my big operation and despite being in a wheelchair I felt very faint. I knew I didn't have time to be wheeled back to bed so I climbed out and put myself on the bathroom floor. The nurse ran off to get a pillow for my head. When she returned I said, "And you know what's happening now!" She quickly grabbed a towel and put it over my 'bits', pushed a big pad under my bum and pulled the other patients' curtains to protect my dignity! I thought it was hilarious and produced the poo of my life! When she lifted the towel, she confirmed it had been very worthwhile. I reminded her to bend her knees as she lifted the beast!

PART 66

It's Sunday 28th December – which is actually the day I thought I would be leaving hospital. In reality I left Christmas Eve, although absolutely nothing feels real about that! Mum went home on the Monday and phoned to say she would be with me Christmas Day – that was her target and I felt really fortunate that we would be together and would both be well enough to enjoy it. I love Christmas and this year wasn't any less exciting – it was just going to be different. But the day before Christmas Eve Mr Italian Man talked me through everything and explained they were going to slow down for a few weeks and give me time to heal. Therefore there was nothing medically to do and if I felt up to it, I could go home. I was confused and scared, but he reassured me I was out of the danger period and I just needed to rest. He thought Christmas at home was the best option. So I talked it over with Tim and, through liaison with his mum and Richard, a Christmas Day plan was hatched. Christmas Eve arrived and I passed all the discharge tests given to me by physios and OTs and I was off, first stop had to be my favourite curry house. Not only is the fish curry the food of this champion it is most definitely a 'super' food designed to boost my recovery! We text a few friends/family and 11 of us sat down to an early dinner. Pretty surreal of course, but pretty natural for us!!

Then Christmas Day arrived and it was unbelievable! It was so normal. Mum, Dad and Rich pitched up with full festive head gear and being together began. We had a full lunch including all the usual trimmings, we opened lots of presents, we chatted, we ate a Christmas tea, we Skyped a few people and we enjoyed each other's company. Mum was better than I had hoped for and I think she surprised everyone including herself. They thought they were just popping over for a couple of hours to have a snack, so staying for two full meals and leaving at 9pm was way beyond their expectations. Dad was a bit wobbly. I think he was in shock that everything felt so normal. He doesn't seem to understand his own emotions at the moment, so his comments can seem very negative. I struggle with that. Any negativity now makes me cross. We have come so far. We are doing so well. Now I do not count my chickens, far from it, but I do think we should feel grateful for where we are and at that particular time – Christmas Day – we were all together, at home, feeling pretty healthy and for me that's definitely worth celebrating! We had fun. We really did. And apart from Mum feeling weak, me having one eye and a big scar across my head and neither of us having a proper drink, it felt normal but special at the same time. The day flew by. It really was quite unbelievable. I just can't process it!

PART 67

This was written by a triathlon buddy in New Zealand

for her local newspaper – I had no idea but feel very proud – thank you!

This is a brilliantly timely daily post.

My unsung hero is going to remain nameless. That's because they are the kind of person who doesn't like drawing attention to themself. They don't ask for thanks, or help, they just do what they do.

This person has fought a few battles, some of which I am sure I don't even know about. They first made themselves known to me when I first faced the knee problems that eventually ended my triathlon career. This person also had similar problems. They had not let it stop them. In fact, they were still winning races regardless. It made me wonder what might have been possible for them, had they not had the limitations that were placed upon them.

They have never complained, always smile, always look cheerful and positive. I often wonder how they do it.

They are currently battling a life-threatening illness. Despite this, they remain forward focused and goal driven, speaking of future work commitments and recent promotions.

They are ever giving, meeting the needs of others, whilst privately scaffolding their own support structures to help them continue to battle life.

They never waste a moment, value everything, wish for nothing. They have been the creator of their own destiny, despite the curve balls life has thrown at them.

I bet if this person read this, they wouldn't think that what they were doing was anything special. They have said they aren't in fact brave, they are just doing the best that they can.

That is all you can ask of yourself, or anyone in this world.

My Hero

PART 68

So everything was going so well. Apart from my eye and face numbness I felt pretty much 'normal'. I didn't feel ready to train or anything, but on the whole I felt good. Then just over a week ago my positivity started to slide. I couldn't put my finger on anything in particular, but I just felt a bit low. I headed to bed to give it some thought and it came to me in a flash. It was New Year's Eve. It was time for reflection. It was time to make resolutions and plan and that was making me sad. A year ago I made a life-changing decision to go part time at school – and I did. But that happiness was short lived with my diagnosis. Then with my operation scheduled for December I'd planned to start 2015 free from Tooties and ready to hit everything hard. Only removing 50% of Tooties, finding my compromised carotid artery and losing the sight in one eye weren't in my plans. Going into 2015 not knowing if a) I needed another big op and/or b) radiation therapy meant I didn't know what path I was on and therefore how to approach it. It's like being told you have entered a race but you don't know what distance or when. Do you train for a 5km in spikes or a marathon in gators? I felt disappointed and frustrated. Frustration is a very bad emotion for me because I tend to withdraw and then get angry. It's a no-win situation for those around me. I couldn't make any tangible resolutions so I wrote this FB post: "On the face of it we have had a terrible year. Zende died, my mum has been very poorly and of course Tooties reared itself. It would be very easy to push 2014 away and breathe a sigh of relief that it is finally over. But I still can't do that. I can't look back at 2014 with hatred. We have created so many happy memories. I have no regrets. As we move closer to 2015 I know we have more challenges ahead. Perhaps radiotherapy. Perhaps a second operation. Perhaps both. I may be visually impaired. My life may never be the same. But those are all ifs and maybes. What I know for sure is that I am loved and I know how to love. Whatever happens I will be OK and we will make even more happy memories. It won't be the same. It will be different, but different doesn't have to mean worse. It can be great again, just in a different way. So FB friends, none of us knows what 2015 will bring, but please embrace it, live it and believe in yourself. Happiness is a choice. You deserve it. Happy New Year. "God bless" xx. This was my way of trying to get some perspective and lift myself out of the funk. Then on January 2nd I woke with a terrible headache and horrible nausea. I couldn't even face drinking. I slept most of the day. Tim phoned the hospital and spoke to my nurse and my registrar. They tried to reassure me and invited me back for tests the next day.

So back to Southmead we went. I had a bag packed because I fully expected to stay. Mr Italian Man was there and we had a chat. He said that because he had seen me he wasn't worried. He even dissuaded me from having another scan and blood tests. He simply said that what I was experiencing was normal and that I just needed to accept what a massive ordeal I'd been through and take time to recover. Now you might think "what a waste of time" but it really wasn't, because during our chat we asked a few questions and suddenly things became clearer. He revealed that they weren't planning a carotid artery reconstruction at this stage because they think I was born with a small carotid. Tooties had nothing to do with it! He also confirmed they weren't planning to operate or radiate the remaining 50%. I will just be scanned annually and any treatment will be decided based on any changes. For now, he said my sight was their focus.

When we left Tim was very emotional. He was overjoyed that he wouldn't have to see me go through more pain and risk. He felt overwhelming relief. But I didn't. It was strange really. Mr Italian Man had just told me I could start planning. He had put me on my path and yet I still felt low. Tim couldn't understand and I struggled to articulate it, but having had time to think about it, I felt disappointed. Tooties will always cast a shadow. I wanted it out. I wanted to have that moment when it was all over. That will never happen. With luck this is the end tumour wise, but only time will tell. A week on and the headaches are a bit better and so is the nausea. I'm eating now, but sporadically and definitely not healthily. I just nailed a 'share bag' of salt and vinegar

crisps – well I didn't believe in sharing when I was well...
I'm going to continue to take it easy, keep taking the pills
and hope that I improve. My nurse did tell Tim that post
operation depression is very common and that it will be
potentially worse for me because I am used to such a
hectic, fitness based lifestyle. I don't buy into this. I feel
low because I feel poorly. It feels worse because I was
feeling so well. I'm not depressed. I know only too well
what that looks like.

PART 69

Now I know I sometimes start a new 'part' apologising for
being away for so long blah blah blah, but hopefully by the
time you finish reading this section you will forgive me!
We went home, I had a sleep and we headed off to
Poole to see Tim's mum and sis and to enjoy some
sea air and a change of scenery. Unfortunately I just
changed beds for 48 hrs! We phoned the hospital every
day when we went home, they prescribed bits and
bobs and continued to try and reassure, but I knew
deep inside it was more. Treating me for constipation
was definitely approaching it from the wrong angle!
So a week later we returned to Southmead. I was so
poorly I couldn't walk. And then the scan revealed
it – a collection on my brain causing pressure and
therefore symptoms. I was admitted and scheduled
for theatre. An unplanned operation was imminent
as soon as they could collate enough information.
They performed my procedure Sunday morning.
And that was supposed to be that. The gunk was sent for
analysis and I began treatment for an infection. I was on a

normal neuro ward and felt pretty OK until 48 hours later. I will always remember lying there and realising I was actually fighting for my life. I was taken to ICU and the atmosphere around me was very bleak. They didn't know what was happening to me. My temperature shot up to 41.9° and my blood pressure plummeted to 83/51. They couldn't understand why I wasn't in a coma! And then the main man said those immortal words; "Put Rachel nil by mouth." I shot upright in my bed, "Not another operation!" I shouted. "It's not fair!" And that was really the first time I had felt this way. Fortunately I was put on 30 min observations and the decision was made to monitor me closely for a week and see how I responded to the drugs, unless I deteriorated further. It's been a bit up and down if I'm honest. It's mostly linked to sleep and food, but I'm beginning to have more good hours than bad.

And anyway, this horror is worth it. I'm happy to go through this! "How ridiculous" I hear you say! "Why would you say such a stupid thing? That Tooties really has messed up your brain!" Why do I say this? Because my mum has been here! The infection has given her a second chance. She is coping and is proving to herself that she can be strong and in control. I am proud of her!

I've decided on my commemorative tattoo. The big tattoo decision has been made. I now know the design and location. As soon as I'm home I'm going to book it. It will be very special and will show everyone how grateful I am for everything I have had and will have. It will represent this time in my life. You see this has happened. The tattoo is for life, but so too are the memories. I remember all the good stuff and all the bad stuff. The good stuff obviously keeps me positive. The bad stuff just makes me dig deeper. Tooties was joined by Puss Pot, but even with an accomplice it couldn't beat me, proving that I am tougher than tough! X

Part 70

Following an incredibly rough week, I've had too much time to think in some respects, but in others I've been able to really see myself.

I did literally fight for my life and that wasn't in the plan! I was supposed to have a major op and then recover. I wasn't supposed to be ill. And I've been so poorly. Of course my infection is rare and has taken ages to identify and the treatment is very aggressive. The drugs are so toxic it's nearly as bad as having chemotherapy and the side effects are very similar to my infection's symptoms. It's confusing and frightening. Technically I'm improving but I don't feel any better!

Part 71

Shart Attack! Most of you will be familiar with the term 'shart', but for any of you with more sophisticated lives it means a cross between a fart and a shit! Well with my infection medication it is never safe to assume that a fart will always be a fart! And bearing in mind there are times when I can't actually move myself properly I often ask,

"Tim have I done a shart?" I asked Nik once but she passed the job onto Tim. Now that's love!

Part 72

This isn't an easy write. I have had some very dark thoughts and I know anyone who loves me will find this very difficult to read.

It's like I've become the lead role in the film 'Lucy' minus the Chinese gangsters plus an overwhelming nausea. Every sense is heightened. I can't bear noise and light. The buzzers literally screech through me and are making my head worse. I have a repellent sweet taste in my mouth which stops me eating too. I can't stand the thought or smell of coffee. My toiletries disgust me. I even hate my own fingernails. I will never bite them again! Tim's beard made me feel queasy when he kissed me. The sound of my dad eating... the list goes on and on. And there seems to be no end. And then the dark thoughts come: What if they can't cure me? What if the infection can only be controlled and this is it? Basically Rachel Bown would be gone. I couldn't work, I couldn't do anything. It would be worse than having a 'normal disability'. I could learn to adapt to that, but this nausea is unbearable. Mix that with the loss of my right eye and 'I have to be honest' I can't see why or how I could live. I'm 44 years old and I'm struggling with the thought of another six weeks like this. I love Tim and my family so much and I know they would be devastated to be without me, but that was the 'me' before. Suicide is a selfish act, but I know I can't live another 30 years like this. I'm scared of death but I'm also terrified of living like this.

Basically at the moment I'm running out of coping strategies. I can't sleep. I can't eat. My head spins with thoughts. I try to push them away, but they come out in nightmares when I do eventually sleep. I miss Little Big Murph so much now it hurts in my chest. I'm tearful for the first time since this whole episode of my life began. Tim sent me a beautiful text: "You have become quite obsessed with raising yourself and improving for other people. The reason why everyone is so supportive of you is because they have no expectations of you. All you have to do is stay in for the ride. This is an Ironman not a sprint. You got a cramp in your calf in the swim, you chaffed in mile two on the bike and you will blister at mile three in the marathon. Right now you're halfway through the bike. Yes you're miserable, yes it seems a challenge too far, but you know what? You will finish. Forget about raising yourself. Get your head down and dig in. I love you more than I could ever tell you and all I'm focused on is the finish line which will come sooner than you think. Just let your fitness take over for now and give your thoughts a rest." I know he is right, but I just feel so poorly. I'm frustrated because it's not how it should be. I expected a long recovery in or out of hospital following a 12 hour brain surgery, but I wasn't supposed to be poorly with it. If I didn't feel sick I could recover better. I could eat and drink and go for little walks. I could get stronger physically and mentally. At the moment I am stuck in bed with the start of pressure sores and the promise of more nausea. There is nothing I can do to help myself or change anything. I came into hospital feeling happy and well and six weeks later I feel doomed. This is my latest race analogy: I started an ultra marathon.

I knew it was the longest event of my life but I knew the route and I knew where the finish was. I'd split it up into chunks and it didn't really phase me. The race started and I found myself in the lead. I passed through aid stations and felt really good. The crowd couldn't believe how well I was doing and it looked like I was on for a course record. But then a race saboteur moved a crucial sign and because I was so far ahead no-one else noticed. I kept going. I had a feeling something was wrong, but continued anyway. I was in the middle of nowhere, before I collapsed with exhaustion. I needed help. A kind old lady appeared and gave me some food and water. She couldn't drive and didn't have a telephone. She explained there was no short cut back or alternative route. I would just need to turn round, re-trace my steps and start again. It was starting to rain and get dark. I cried. How could I keep going?

And that I suppose is where I am now. I'm searching for a little bit of company in my lonely head. I'm desperate to find food and water that will sustain my trip back. I don't mind starting again, even though I know I will be well behind. I don't expect to catch up. I just want to be back on the right course, with the crowd and other runners around me. I just want to know that by putting one foot in front of the other I am making progress. And that's that.

Part 73

Ten days later

I awoke with the news that "You can go home today!" It came as a bit of a shock, so I immediately started asking questions that I didn't really want to know the answers to! What happens if in five weeks, time the infection hasn't cleared? Reading between the lines, they will operate again to replace my false graft with something from my own body (chest or leg) because that's the bit that is most likely to hold onto the bugs. If this is the news, I'm pretty sure I will be hysterical! I will be three months in and back to square one if not even further back than that. In a way it's too much to comprehend. I'm not being negative, I just can't cope with the possibility. But for now I am grateful that I can go home and be with Tim and LBM. I need to rest and give the pills the best chance I can. I can eat good nutritious food, relax properly in comfort and hopefully fight this infection. I will say my prayers and hope that I am granted the strength to be well both physically and mentally. I'm scared, worried, frustrated – I could use many more negative descriptives, but I need to embrace hope. I need to be the leper, the blind man, the cripple and let Jesus heal me. I must hold my faith. X

Part 74

It's now four weeks since my second operation and nine days since I came home. I've resisted writing before today because I really wanted to order my thoughts and feel confident about what I was trying to say.

The difficulty I have had is that I spent five out of seven weeks in hospital and in that time I nearly died. So when everyone started messaging or saying 'Oh it must feel great to be home' the reality was – it didn't! At first I didn't understand why and I felt bad inside for Tim and my family. But then I realised I'd become institutionalised. I had felt safe in the day to day routines of the hospital. I liked the continuous monitoring and routines. I knew what each day looked like and the doctors and nurses were always there to reassure. At home I felt vulnerable and I realised I was scared of everything. I started to worry that I was going to be attacked, that people were going to break into the house, that Little Big Murph was going to be dog-napped. The reason for these thoughts? For the first time in my life I didn't feel invincible. I've always thought I could defend myself enough to save my life or to run away. But now I felt weak, poorly and helpless and that terrified me.

And this continued for a few days. I couldn't be left on my own. I was even having palpitations which Mum told me were probably linked subconsciously to anxiety. I wouldn't even shower without Tim watching me (he said he didn't mind as he hadn't seen me naked for months!) But then we hired a wheelchair and I began to go out. On day one Tim pushed me all the way. On day two I walked about 200m. On day three we took the chair but I didn't sit in it and on day four we didn't even take it. And then I decided I didn't need it. I was strong and confident enough not to need it.

So as I sit here writing this, how do I feel now? Of course I still feel vulnerable, but we have padlocked the back gate and I have been left through parts of the day and night. Tim has to work and I have to start re-integrating myself back into 'normal' life. I can now do simple household stuff like washing up and making dinner. Only a week ago those things were impossible. So I have made huge progress since I came home. I am now halfway through my antibiotic treatment plan and I'm getting used to it. The side effects aren't limiting me like they were. I am adapting.

And the BIG news! The first sign of hope suddenly appeared. My eye started to twitch and showed signs of trying to open! Yes, it's only a millimetre if that, but it is definitely moving. I cried with excitement. Could it be, that after everything I have been through I might reappear on the other side looking pretty much how I used to look? Could I be the blind man in Jesus's story? Let's pray.

PART 75

Once again it's been a while since I wrote anything. It's been a combination of being very busy and just not feeling ready to write. Ironically as my eye has continued to open my well-being has declined. I have felt more tired and headachy and as a result my mood has been very up and down. Tim and those around me try to reassure me and rationalise what's going on, but I feel like they are trying to rationalise the irrational! When Mr Italian Man confirmed my blood was "remarkable" I was very happy but still not completely trusting. Until the MRI confirms everything is normal and until I am able to restart my fitness regime I just can't relax and enjoy any results. I need it to be over. Progress isn't enough because I have made that before and then been kicked in the fanny. I'm also getting close to the point where I am either 'well' or having another operation. The gap between the two is too huge to imagine and I fear my reaction and ability to cope if it's the latter. I also think about how Tim and my family will cope. We have all been through so much. I know my path is set and God already knows my destination, but I still pray for the easy route. I can't help but feel like we deserve a break and deserve to breathe again.

PART 76

Some people can be sooo rude! Now I sometimes misjudge people. I'm sure we all do, but if I had had to guess what sort of person would send me into a 'blind' rage (excuse the pun) over my disability, I wouldn't have predicted it would be a middle-aged retired man I was meeting for the first time.

Tim had a meeting in a nice place to walk Murph, so we tagged along. When I got out of the car wearing my bandana because it was cold and my eye patch because I can't see without it (due to the eye opening slightly and causing double vision), said man randomly shouts, "I won't make any jokes yet!" Now bear in mind, he hasn't been introduced and has never clapped his fully functioning eyes on me before! I was livid. I was so cross I grabbed Murph and walked in the opposite direction. I didn't want to embarrass Tim, but I was ready to explode. How incredibly rude!

When I finally calmed down I felt very low. Through my teaching career and football career I had never been insulted about my appearance or had my leg pulled about anything physical. I had never had any outstanding features, like a big nose or sticky out ears. And in that moment, that one comment made me feel like a sitting duck for ridicule and prejudice. I realised that I did look different to everyone else, that I did draw unwanted attention and second looks and that I probably always would. I also realised that until that point everyone around me had been promoting my self image and shielding me from my reality. They all still complimented me and told me how well I looked and how strong and amazing I was being. He crushed that. He made me feel like a freak. He made me question myself. He made me realise I am different and for that period of time I couldn't spin it in a positive way. The only emotions I could muster were either sadness or rage and for my own mental health, rage felt better!

PART 77

Very sadly one of my parents' neighbours died in distressing circumstances and it really affected me. Before Tooties I know it would have registered with me but I don't think it would have had such a big impact. It was one of the worst situations I have ever witnessed and it has consumed me for a few days. I now realise my reaction is because it felt too close to home and I don't mean my parents' house! I have looked Death and Desperation in the face and flicked them the bird! I have realised that I am now a different person. I am more sensitive to illness and the impact it has on everyone. I don't take my health and fitness for granted – I can't imagine I ever will again.

Part 78

This has been a big week. I went out for the first time on my own and in true Rachel Bown style I didn't exactly ease myself in gently! I didn't just pop across the road to the garage, or walk Murph around the block, no that would be too obvious. I decided to venture to the Westfield Shopping Centre in London! Oh and I also decided to catch a bus and spend five hours there whilst Tim was at work! How did it go? Honestly – I was terrified! To begin with I took ages to cross a busy road. Then when my bus arrived I wasn't allowed on because I didn't have an Oyster card. That was nearly enough to completely spook me, but fortunately when another bus arrived and I asked the driver where I could get an Oyster card from, he took pity on me and let me travel for free. I was overwhelmed by his kindness and it gave me strength.

That strength lasted a few minutes! An older man started staring at me and then moved closer. He pointed at my eye patch and started asking questions. I felt vulnerable and suspicious. When he got off I felt relieved but sad that my new lack of confidence mistook his friendliness for something more sinister. I told myself off and tried to convince myself shopping would make me feel more like myself, but it didn't.

Really it was a step too far. It was too busy, too noisy and just too much. I felt like everyone was staring at me and again I felt vulnerable. I felt like everyone could see my defences were down and that I would be picked out as an easy target. I also felt exhausted. So I made a plan. I would visit a few shops and then sit down for a drink. Then a few more followed by lunch. And that's how I passed the time. I spent more time sitting and thinking than actually shopping, but in that time I realised that, despite how I felt, I was coping. Yes it was tough, but I was doing it and I was saving more money than a typical shopping trip because I limited where I looked! I also grabbed some perspective by remembering that only three weeks before I was still in hospital!

PART 79

It was just as well I saved some cash in London because the next day turned out to be an unexpectedly expensive one! We visited the Bristol Eye Hospital, where we were basically told I have very limited vision in my right eye, which combined with third nerve damage, means I have severe double vision which can't be corrected and may or may not improve naturally. In short it may improve cosmetically but is unlikely to improve practically and if it does or it doesn't I need special glasses. Or as I have been, I can wear a patch. Now the patch has caused me some problems. It becomes uncomfortable and despite choosing cool girly designs, it draws attention, which in turn makes me anxious. So when the doctor suggested I wore glasses and frosted out the right lens, I was happy to try. But the pair she gave me were not cool and not designer, so of course there was only one solution – go and order three pairs of cool designer glasses! In the meantime we taped up a pair of Oakleys and a pair of fashion sunnies, and do you know what? When I went to Chippenham to meet Mum for lunch, I walked down the high street and felt normal for the first time since December 15th. No-one could see my eye and I felt confident. For a few minutes I felt like me!

Part 80

A good friend visited today. I hadn't seen her since just after my first operation and as I re-told my saga and then explained to her the effect my parents' neighbour's death had had on me, I realised I may be suffering from some kind of Post Traumatic Stress Syndrome. The infection and its consequences mixed with the loss of my sight have been an almighty shock. Neither were planned for and until recently neither have been fully understood. And because I still haven't come through the other side and won't know any outcomes for an unknown period, I still can't find closure and I can't come to terms with it all. I know I need to be a patient patient and I know it's early days, but I relive it all again and again. I remember minute details. I see images. I look deep into myself and question everything. I feel everyone's pain and worry. I pray for the strength to get through. I want to be well and I know my mental health and physical health are locked together. I am an athlete. I need to sweat and hurt physically to heal my emotional pain. I need to rebuild my fitness to rebuild my confidence. I need to bury my memories in a heap of dirty training kit. I need to fight back!

Part 1. Kitzbühel European Sprint Triathlon Championships 2014. This picture shows every sinew in my body and every bit of my personality reaching for the line. Little did I know that less than 2 weeks later I would be competing against the most difficult opponent of my life!

Part 3. One of the best days of my life. Best woman for my favourite girlie couple.

Part 28. Digging for gold!

Part 58. Tim shaving my hair before my first operation.

Part 58. At Southmead hospital.

Part 60. With Tim.

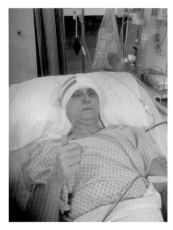

Part 61. Intensive Care
"Thumbs up, I'm OK everyone!"

Part 61. Both
still smiling.

Part 74. My first trip out with
Little Big Murph following my
second operation.

*Part 82. My first run/walk
March 1st 2015.*

*Part 85. Best friend
Marsha and I on my
first bike ride following
treatment.*

*Part 91. Proud to
be an ambassador
for Brain Tumour
Support.*

Part 92. Racing again with dear friend Neil, April 2015.

Part 104. Team Abrams. Always great fun!

Part 107. Eilat Olympic Distance European Championships 2012. My first International medal.

Part 107. European Champion 2013 by 1 second!

Part 108. The proudest day of my life. The Olympic Torch Relay 2012.

Part 117. Proud of this 'Sporting Champion!'

Part 121. Geneva European Sprint Triathlon Championships 2015. So happy to be representing my country.

PART 81

Today was Tim's birthday and we planned to have a nice walk with LBM and then a curry at our favourite Indian restaurant thanks to a generous voucher from my mum and dad. I suggested we went somewhere a bit different for our walk and so I chose my favourite place to run. Over the last couple of years I have spent many miles and many hours running along the Kennet and Avon Canal Towpath. Rain or shine, light or dark (with a head torch!) it's my favourite place to run. Murph can run off the lead. I can do consistent efforts, run out and back negative splits, run an even pace or go on some great off-road loops. For me it's the perfect location whatever my training program says.

So that's where I wanted to go today. The sun was shining, it was pretty warm and I was glad to be back. You see I made a decision yesterday. With only eight days of antibiotics to go I decided that from the 1st March I will start my physical rehabilitation which in turn will trigger my emotional rehabilitation. I wanted to see how I felt being in my favourite place as a different person, with different abilities. I decided that waiting for the day when my head feels 'normal' may never come. How I feel now may be my 'normal'. I may need to adapt to running, cycling and swimming with this fuzzy, numb feeling. I will need to experiment with what I can tolerate. I'm under no illusion that it's going to be quick or easy. I intend to do 6 x 1min jog/4 minutes walk to begin with and build from there. But I am excited about this. I can now picture myself doing it even if my lycra is a bit on the snug side!

So how did I feel after being away for nearly three months? I felt great. I felt comfortable and happy and I felt relieved to be back. I think I even saw Murph smile as he trotted along!

PART 82

Today has been a massive day. I cried today because seven weeks ago I had an emergency second operation. Six weeks ago I was in intensive care and five weeks ago today I didn't know how I could escape the darkness. But today two fabulous things happened: 1) I finished my drug regime 2) I put my lycra on along with my newly printed t-shirt and began my return to fitness. I've been very emotional and pretty overwhelmed. I honestly didn't know if this day would come, but it has and it feels great to be alive!

PART 83

Last night we spent a wonderful evening in a top London restaurant celebrating a very special birthday with my bestie Marsha. The food and company were first class. This morning I jogged/walked for an hour along the Poole-Bournemouth promenade. It was crisp and bright and with Little Big Murph by my side I felt great. As I looked along the beach I reflected on what a lovely evening we had had and how free I felt in the sunshine. These experiences were made all the more relevant when I realised that two months ago tomorrow I nearly died. I'm not saying I don't fight my demons because I do.

My dreams may still be unrealistic and unattainable, but I don't focus on them so much that I ignore the simple pleasures. I do see what I have around me and quite frankly, it's pretty stunning! X"

PART 84

I posted this on Facebook today but it doesn't really tell the full story! In fact it's pretty much a big fat smoke screen probably designed by me to encourage my Facebook fans to blow sunshine up my arse and make me feel better! You see I'm struggling a bit. I feel like a push-me-pull-me situation is being played out in my head. It's easy being poorly. It's even easier to be "inspirational, brave" etc etc when you start to exceed immediate expectations and reach milestones ahead of most other mere mortals! What frightens me is the next stage. What happens in a year's time, when I'm back at work, technically my physical rehabilitation has happened and to all intents and purposes my normal life has resumed? How will I cope with the emotional scars, particularly if I can't push my body to mask the psychological pain in my head? What if I can't be what I was? What if I can't compete at the highest level because my body lets me down? And that's where the conflict starts. I'm thinking about my body failing. I'm criticising its ability. I'm focusing on what it might not allow me to do when in reality this beautiful body, this wonderful machine kept me alive! My dream should now have become a reality. Running along the beach should be my dream come true. All my limbs working in unison. No physical issues other than my sight. But it isn't and I just can't convince myself that it is enough. It is enough today. It will be enough for 2015, but beyond that I know it won't be. I also struggle with people's reactions to me. On the one hand I want sympathy and respect. I want people to recognise and acknowledge what I've been through. I want them to treat me as something special! But then, I resent the same people for pitying me (whether they do or whether I imagine they do is irrelevant!). When we did my first Park Run last weekend I wore my 'Caution Visually Impaired Athlete' t-shirt and people were nice to me. They said nice things – they wound me up! I found their nice comments patronising and as a result I made myself poorly because with 400m to go I abandoned my pacing strategy and thought "Sod it – I am Rachel Bown European Champion 2013 and I am going to show you fat arses who the boss is!"

So I've made two decisions in the last ten days since I began my 'official return to fitness':

1) to race in Geneva at the European Sprint Championships. Of course this does rely on my neuro team giving me the go-ahead, but all things being equal I think it's possible for me to complete the event. I earnt the right to that spot in Kitzbuhel. And because I don't know if I will ever reach a level of fitness to allow me to qualify again, I want to use the opportunity. I also think it is the fairy tale end to this book!

2) I am going to have some counselling. I don't think I need it right now, but I think I should gather some strategies to help me cope with the future and the

potential loss of my sight and physical abilities. I want to be pro-active. I want to deal with potential issues before they engulf me. I can see them lurking in the future and rather hoping everything will be ok, I want to do everything I can to ensure they are ok.

Perhaps I'm over thinking things? My anxieties are probably still based on my lack of control and structure, but hopefully as I get fitter and as my return to work gets closer, my future will become clearer. Only time will tell.

PART 85

My ability to jolt from a positive to a negative mindset in a nanosecond continues to happen. Tim and I talked about it because he had recognised it was happening. He described it as day and night but observed that whatever state I am in I am completely absorbed by it and my thoughts are completely convincing. And that's challenging for both of us – it's hard to keep up with what and how I am thinking. I have to say though, that I have many more positive thoughts than negative ones and I continue to make progress and feel proud of my achievements. Last weekend I jogged the whole of the Bath Skyline Park Run. I changed my game plan and it worked. I still finished in the same time as my previous run/walk attempt but this time I felt strong and happy and above all I wasn't poorly for the next 24 hours. When I realised it was exactly two months since I was rushed to ICU and nearly died it made the day even more special. I have survived and I am adapting and learning about how my body now works.

I've had another first today. I've been out on a bike for the first time since Tooties was tackled. Marsha and I did a lap of Richmond Park on our MTBs. I wore trainers instead of cleats so that I felt more confident about putting my feet down and after a few minutes I forgot I couldn't see with one eye. You see (no pun intended!) as a cyclist you need to be aware and observant anyway, so in the absence of traffic it was the perfect introduction. Yes it was challenging, but I never once thought about how easy it used to be. All I could think about was how great it felt to be out in the sunshine with my best friend, taking my first steps towards becoming a cyclist again.

PART 86

Writing is becoming increasingly difficult and if I'm honest I've been finding excuses not to! As my follow up appointment gets closer I am becoming more and more anxious. On the face of it things are going incredibly well, but ironically that just adds to my angst. Why? Because I'm scared the news from my tests is going to be bad and I'm going to crash back down to Earth with an almighty BANG! I played football for over 20 years and one manager used to say that some players "played with one foot in the dressing room" if they weren't completely focused during the match. That's how I feel. I'm enjoying what I'm doing but I've always got my one eye on the appointment date and am aware that I continually refer to it. In fact I am obsessed with it. I have made some significant progress over the past week but the 'anxiety cloud' still sits above my head and a few days ago it well and truly opened! Actually it happened when we returned home from my day in London with Marsha. Tim and I had a spat. He said I was being mean to him and that he felt he couldn't say or do anything right. He said I had changed in the last two weeks. That I had withdrawn from him. He said I was argumentative and wanted to know why? Being forced to look at myself was horrible. Trying to explain my feelings was near impossible. Everything was mixed up. I felt so confused and I started to cry. Not long ago someone said I must have cried lots in the last eight months. I explained I hadn't because 1) crying made my headache worse and 2) I thought if I started I may not stop! Option 2 came true! I couldn't stop. I sobbed for three hours. I cried because I felt frustrated, worried, frightened, happy, proud, thankful − you name an emotion and I cried about it! And for the first time since I was admitted into hospital on December 10th I slept through the night. That's the first time in over four months! I needed the release. I suppose it was inevitable and although it was difficult for Tim to witness and understand at the time, when we look at it now it was healthy. I'm still worried about my appointment but I definitely feel better in myself. I am definitely more relaxed.

Part 87

Wow! What a BIG weekend and who would have thought two months ago I would have been part of it let alone a BIG part of it?!

It was Tim's New Forest Running Festival. Seven races over a weekend ranging from a 50km Ultra Marathon to a 6km 'Light up the Night' fun run. I decided a few weeks ago when I started to exercise again that I would take part in the fun run and my lovely friend Charlotte agreed to accompany/guide me. The race was due to start at 7pm, but by lunchtime I was bored and itching to do something so I offered to 'sweep' the ladies only 10km. I'm very glad I did. I met a very motivated lady who was participating as a challenge for Lent. She couldn't run because she had injured her knee during training, but was determined to complete the race. We walked and swapped stories. We covered most topics and although she was 20 years my senior our philosophies and outlook on life were very similar. I'm grateful I met her. I will never forget her. She has made an imprint on me. Then it was time for my actual 'race' and oh what fun we had! Charlotte decided to race with baby Nellie in her buggy. That's OK I hear you say, lots of people run with a buggy. Yes they do. But do they run with a buggy off road in the dark in a forest guiding a visually impaired athlete?! Not so much!!! OMG I am still laughing! Nellie was as good as gold. She either sang or slept which considering she is only five months old and was being bumped and bashed around over very rough terrain is a miracle! People couldn't believe there was a real live baby in the buggy! We only had one head torch between us and I was wearing it. Charlotte managed to guide me off piste and we ended up in some bushes. As if that wasn't funny enough, when we turned round we realised four other runners had followed us! I suggested to them that following the blind person in the dark probably wasn't the best idea! They laughed too! Then we got into a race with a dog. Murph and his rival eyeballed one another and I knew Murph wanted to beat it! So we upped the pace. Charlotte did try to remind me it wasn't really a race, but hey who really believes that? So there we are. Flat out into the finish and we did it. I'm sure we won three races in one: 1st baby and buggy, 1st dog and 1st VI athlete. Well it's not our fault no other mummies with buggies or VI athletes wanted to bump around in the dark with us. I've always said "You can only beat who turns up!" Day two of the weekend posed another challenge as I decided to participate in the Open 10km. This would be the longest distance I had jogged/walked. Another lovely friend agreed to accompany/guide me. Sandra Abrams is a legend. She is a fantastic triathlete and races in the 65-69AG proving age isn't a barrier. The plan was to jog the flats and downhills and walk the hills. But Sandra hadn't run for two months, so she couldn't keep up! I waited when Murph had a wee. I waited when Murph had a poo. I waited at a drink station. Eventually Sandra told me to go on. How funny was it when I crossed the finish line and announced I had lost my guide and was going back to find her!! You see we were wearing our VI athlete/guide t-shirts!! Overall it was a fantastic weekend. Tim and his team put on a great event and the feedback was very positive. Once again I probably did a bit too much and I've needed a couple of TV days. I've had my fuzzy head which is a sign I've pushed too hard. But like I've said before, I don't know where the line is until I cross it and I got tired long before I knew Tooties even existed. I may still be playing with one foot in the dressing room but I am trying to stretch my leg as far as possible!

Part 88

I've been left alone over night! For four nights actually! "Oh how exciting" I hear you say with a hint of sarcasm in your voice, but for me it was a major step. Only a few weeks ago I was too scared to be left. I was convinced that someone would break in and murder Murph and that I wouldn't be able to protect us. And because of this I have followed Tim wherever he has gone, obviously wonderful for him! But actually being away so much has been tiring. It has been lovely but I have also missed home, so this week I decided to stay put. I felt it was the right time and it was. I've still been busy, but I have also had time to myself. I haven't been anxious and it's made me realise how strong I am feeling. I'm not convinced I'm a target anymore. I'm obviously feeling less vulnerable and more confident. It's another step along the path to finding the real Rachel Bown.

Part 89

I'm writing this after four pints, whilst really wanting my fifth! It's exactly 24 hours after we have been given the most amazing news – I am no longer a poorly person! Woohoo! Yes, yesterday Mr P's registrar told us I am clear. No more treatment. Unless Tooties changes I won't have to undergo any more treatment. I will be monitored and managed but as far as the neuro team are concerned I am discharged! Unbelievable! I am in total shock. I know I have been feeling well and swimming and biking and running, but I suppose I just didn't dare let myself believe it could be over. History always showed that my body/fitness disguised the real truth. I have been let down and disappointed so often, that to finally be told it's over is actually as big a shock as being told I had a tumour in the first place! I know that sounds bizarre, but it is. But let me tell you, from the minute I left her office I haven't stopped smiling and the really ironic, strange thing is that despite the fact I have run for 30 minutes and biked for over two hours today, fuzzy head hasn't made an appearance! Strange hey? The registrar was surprised I was running, swimming and biking only 10 weeks after puss pot was evacuated, but she simply said, "Listen to your body and do what you feel you can," and I am! I'm exercising, eating and drinking! I have decided to party hard over Easter and then I will lock down until the Euros. I won't be taking the race seriously, but I will control the controllables and eating and drinking come under that banner. Let's be honest, the photos are vital. I've got half a stone to lose! They will feature in the last part of this book. The final part will be written after I race in Geneva. As I've always said, my life race finishes when I begin the next significant race and that race my friends is in Geneva on the 10th July 2015 and I can't wait!! X

Part 90

So how do I feel a few days on from such fabulous news? I honestly don't think I have stopped smiling. I think I even smile in my sleep! I'm tired, but I have been partying! I've eaten more chocolate and sweet stuff and drank more alcohol in a few

days than I probably did in the whole of 2014.
For six months I had a cloud above my head. For four
months I was caught in the storm and then last Thursday
evening the sun came out again and it has never shone
brighter! X

So Tooties didn't win!

Let's be honest that Mother Trucker tumour never stood
a chance
Cos this action lady was made to last!
The odds were never in its favour
Team Peace Bown were never going to waver

But Tooties had a secret accomplice
A stinky infection that tried to spoil our bliss

Puss Pot made me very poorly
Sending my temperature way over forty

I very nearly died
And for the first time I even cried

But Tooties and Puss Pot's time was always limited
Pain and anguish would never be enough to win it.

Love and resilience, patience and strength
Trust, faith and respect will go to any length.

It nearly was a very sad ending,
But as we now know, it was just the beginning!

PART 91

Today is a strange day. It's the start of the next 'post Tooties' phase, but once again I'm battling the chimp on my shoulder! We attended the Meningioma Awareness Day yesterday and it was great. I met lots of people who have had similar experiences and I was able to show my gratitude to the neuro team. I gave Mr P lots of hugs and I felt very comfortable sharing my story. Another patient and I talked to the group and I felt happy to have been asked to do so. I also felt very proud when people told me they enjoyed my speech and found me inspirational. Things got even better when the Brain Tumour Support charity founder asked me to be an ambassador for them! Exciting times and without much effort my dream of becoming a public speaker and helping others to see beyond their diagnosis has started to become a reality. We are talking about websites and fundraising and we are putting a plan together starting with my 'Life Party'. So why the conflict? I feel and am fat! Yes folks I'm heavier than I have ever been and I can see fat! I have put half a stone of pure lard on in three weeks! Yes three weeks. Obviously I know what happened. In the weeks leading up to my big hospital appointment I thought 'sod it, I could be back in hospital soon!' and then after the big appointment I thought 'sod it, I'm celebrating!' Copious amounts of pudding, chocolate and beer have done the damage, so I'm not in denial about how I reached this point, but now I'm here, I hate it! This gives the chimp free reign and it chips away at me. In reality I know that I'm in great shape considering what I've been through, but I'm a bit sick of legitimising everything in this way and anyway the simple fact of the matter is I don't like feeling fat and being fat. It's time to take control of what I put in. After all, I'm a fraud if I stand up in front of an audience and say "life is wonderful if I know I'm hiding a secret bulge!" It's also bloody hard to run and bike at this weight. I have exactly 3 months until Geneva. I aim to lose a lb a week. I won't get there race fit but I can be leaner than I am now. Yesterday Mr P said that if I could get within 20% of where I used to be then I was extraordinary! That's my goal. I will love the event, but I also want to send him a photo of me crossing the finishing line with the heading 'extraordinary' because that's my way of really saying "thank you" to him. I didn't say everything I wanted to say yesterday because everyone was post-op and coping as best they could with the outcome, but what I will say to pre-op patients in the future is this: our operations and care cost hundreds of thousands of pounds. Every one of us deserves it because we are worth it, but we owe it to ourselves, our families and the neuro team to live our lives positively and productively following surgery. Not everyone can be a GB triathlete, but everyone can be the best they can be. Our brains will always be fighting our tumours or coping with radiation damage, but we cannot afford to worry about the future all the time. For now we need to really live our lives and above all hang onto the only thing we really have – hope!

PART 92

One of the problems (of which there are a few!) with brain surgery is that no-one can tell you anything for sure. Should I be worried about XYZ? Is 'such and such' normal? Mix that with Rachel Bown and things can get pretty complicated! I have felt pretty rough for three days, so deciding to run the Corsham 10km was a difficult decision. But I did feel slightly better and I rationalised that if I was making the wrong decision my body would show me very quickly. When I entered I set myself a target of sub 60 minutes, but I reassessed this and decided that to just finish feeling ok, would be fine!

I started apprehensively and monitored every step. How was I feeling? Was anything unusual happening? At 4km I felt pretty rubbish. In fact I felt really sick, but the feeling wasn't changing or getting worse and suddenly I found my confidence. Later my guide Neil described the change "as a cloud lifting!" I relaxed and began to enjoy it.

We didn't run all the way. I walked the hills and stopped to have a proper drink. I even celebrated getting a blister at 9km. After all, at one stage only a few months ago I didn't know if I would ever earn a blister again!

My finishing time was just over 57 minutes and I haven't felt any worse for racing. Even if it does turn out to be the wrong decision physically, it will always be the right one mentally. Seize the day and enjoy what you can when you can. Life cannot be all 'ifs, buts and maybes!'

Part 93

This part was worth writing because three significant milestones have been reached or remembered this week. We have come to London to visit the marathon exhibition. That in itself is not unusual, I come every year whether I'm participating or not! What is significant though is this: 1) when we came to London in February I was terrified. I felt vulnerable and weak both physically and mentally. In fact I was so frightened something bad would happen to me I spent most of the day sat in a coffee shop wishing the time away, desperate for Tim to finish work. Today I went for a run and went on the underground to the Excel on my own. What a difference! 2) I tried to put the same trousers on that I wore on our last London trip – I couldn't get them on! Yep, high living and celebrating has definitely caught up. The scales had warned me, but now my clothes are telling me! Half a stone to lose. 3) I'm a big anniversary person. I pretty much remember the date of anything and everything regardless of whether it's happy, sad or indifferent! So what did we celebrate last night? Well, we went back to our favourite restaurant and had a toast to my first 'episode'. Yes a year ago this week after we had visited the London Marathon exhibition, had a run in Hyde Park and eaten and drank far too much at Halepi, I experienced my first big headache and eye palsy. I remember it very vividly because I thought I was more drunk than I'd realised and so didn't even tell Tim! We were watching a film and he asked if I was going to sleep? I said, "No I'm watching the film," and he replied, "What with your eyes closed?" I did drift off to sleep and the next morning I was fine. So who could have predicted what was to come? So much has happened since the last London Marathon and no doubt a lot will happen before the next one. Fingers crossed I will be on the start line with thousands of pounds of sponsorship money waiting for me at the finish!

Part 94

Today felt like a very significant day. It was my first hair cut since my operations and my first colour since my diagnosis. I've been looking forward to it for ages. You see my dark hair had become synonymous with being poorly. Lots of people said kind things about my dark hair, how lucky I was to not be grey etc, but it made me sad. Not having a choice and not using my 'products' made me feel different. Even Tim said he hadn't realised how much my hair represented my personality and how he missed seeing a little blonde head bobbing towards him in a crowd! As it turns out the colour was actually more important to me than the length. I didn't mind Tim shaving it off, it actually felt lovely and I didn't mind seeing my scar. Funny, I accepted and embraced that. But now I am back to looking like me and I feel great!

Part 95

Who would have thought I could be this excited? Who would have thought I would cry, again? What has made me excited and tearful? A phone call that's what! A phone call that has confirmed Occupational Health think I am fit to return to work! Now I know that this sounds like madness. That that bloody tumour must have really affected my brain, but honestly I am sane and rational and oh so happy. I am nearly back to being me! When I walk into that hall and see those faces sat on that bench waiting for me to play my warm up music I will know it's actually over. I will have officially won. I will have officially smashed Tooties and Puss Pot into oblivion and into my past! This is another great day!

Part 96

I can't sleep – I'm just too happy! If I could attach a theme tune to this entry you would be hearing Pharell's 'Happy' in the background! Everything is flying around in my head, but it's all good. As I've said before, dates and anniversaries are never wasted on me and I've just realised that my return to work date is exactly five months from my finishing date! I left school on the 5th December and I am returning on the 5th May. Mr Porter told me to wipe away a year of my life, but I think five months is plenty! I'm so excited about my future. There is sooooo much to look forward to. This is what I am going to put in my Facebook post tomorrow when I have given my Headteacher the good news. I'm bursting to post it now but I know I should tell him first! "So Facebook family, it is over. I have been given the thumbs up from the Occupational Health team to return to work – next week! That means our lives are going back to normal and Tooties and Puss Pot have been smashed into the past. I will be having a phased return and it starts exactly five months to the day! I'd like to thank you all for supporting Tim and I. From my diagnosis last June, through my two operations and during my recovery you have been truly wonderful. I also want to mention my school. I'm not supposed to name it, but I do get up like a Lark and watch the sun Rise! My Headteacher, Deputy Head and Governing Body have looked after me from D-Day. Within an hour of my life-changing phone call they were behind me. I have never felt so valued and respected and for that I will always be grateful. And last, but by all means never least, I need to publically thank Tim, my mum and dad, Richard and Ronnie and Tim's family for loving and supporting me and one another. As I said to Tim on Valentine's Day "Individually we are strong, but together we are truly a force of nature!" The fight has been fought, the race has been raced and Team Peace Bown have crossed the line triumphant. We have won!"

PART 97

I've had a very philosophical day today. I have been out on my bike by myself and have had time to reflect and think. I've shared my thoughts with my counsellor and she says they are all very profound but also very enlightening and positive. I've had four sessions with her now. To begin with I just wanted to know if I was likely to suffer from PTSD at some point in the future and how to cope with people 'forgetting' what I have been through. She doesn't think I will suffer with PTSD because I consciously take myself back to my dark days in order to measure my progress and celebrate how far I have come. Apparently PTSD sufferers don't have a choice with their thoughts and they always imagine it is going to happen again or is happening again. They don't have a choice and everything is negative. And as for moving forwards and forgetting, I see this very differently now, because so many doors are opening and because I want to help others, my story will never be forgotten. I can see myself in ten years time, standing in front of a group of people and saying, "My name is Rachel Bown. Ten years ago I had a brain tumour removed, but look at what I have achieved since...!" The longer I tell my story and the more I do the more significant it becomes. It will show others that this was not a point in time when I stopped, it was really the point in time when I started!

We also explored the idea that my feelings and ambitions might be ego driven. Everyone likes to be praised and at the moment I am constantly having smoke blown up my arse! Every day someone tells me how well I'm doing, how inspirational I am etc etc. And because this is so lovely I questioned if this was the real reason I wanted to keep my story alive. We agreed it wasn't (phew, I'm not such a big head after all!). The counsellor guided me through a range of scenarios and different situations and every time I reached the same conclusion. I want my message to be heard because I want to help people be the best they can be. From the kids I teach through to patients that have just been diagnosed, I want to help them achieve. Of course I'd like everyone to like me, but if my messages offend... I'd rather be respected than liked. Fundamentally I have a passion and that is to share my experiences so that as many people as possible make the most of what they have. I absolutely believe that I can make a difference and apparently that means I am not dictated to by my ego!

My life was full and vibrant before Tooties. I had achieved a lot. I was happy, but looking back it was comfortable and I pretty much knew what the future looked like. Now it's exciting and fresh. I am like a magpie. I want to collect every opportunity and do it NOW! But I know I need to be patient. I'm not even 50% of the way through my recovery, but I still want to do it NOW. This can be a bit difficult for those close to me because I am adrenalin fuelled and totally driven by excitement. They are still knackered and recovering from the ordeal. It's hard for them to keep up!

PART 98 – MY FIRST RACE!

This actually happened a little bit earlier than planned. With a weeks' notice I found myself in a local triathlon. I had entered a couple of novice races but they were both open water and it suddenly dawned on me it might be a bit more progressive to enter a pool based race first. My local newspaper had followed my triathlon career and so they were keen to cover 'the comeback race story'. Well you would have thought they could at least photoshop the photos to hide the fact I'm not exactly lean at the moment, how rude!

I knew I could complete the individual sections (400m/25k/5k) but stringing them together was going to be the challenge. The other less fitness based challenge was how I would actually get from the pool to transition without bumping into anyone or anything! The solution to this problem was obvious, swallow my pride and run around the sports centre with my goggles on! (One side is taped up so I don't suffer with double vision) Of course I would look like a) a complete novice or b) a complete nutter but at least I wouldn't be crashing into anything!

I loved it. I smiled throughout. I even sang to myself on

the bike. I swam as if nothing had ever happened. Maybe there is a message in that? I biked too hard but didn't care. I knew I was over cooking it but it felt fabulous to go fast. And then came the run or should I say shuffle?! But I just didn't care. It was horrible to feel so sluggish. My body wouldn't go any faster. Someone told me to think about the pain I had suffered in hospital, but my legs wouldn't respond to any psychological motivation, but I didn't care. I was doing it! I was in a race less than four months after my second operation. My body wasn't letting me down it was proving itself to the world (well Trowbridge at any rate) and so I was winning.

Later when we looked at the results I had finished 3rd in my category and spookily I had finished exactly 20% behind the time I had won the same race two years previously. Remember that was the target Mr Porter had set me and I had already achieved it. But being 20% behind is not what should really be celebrated. The real achievement is that in less than four months I have made an 80% improvement. I have literally gone from lying in an ICU bed to crossing a finishing line in just a few weeks. And boy, am I proud of that!

PART 99

What a way to go back. My first day back at work was almost a mirror image of what I was doing at a similar time last year. There is a big difference though – Tooties isn't with me and I'm not scared. I'd just been diagnosed before the last Youth Sport Trust conference and although I still loved it I was obviously very distracted. I didn't know what was going to happen and I remember feeling very different to everyone else in the room.

A year on and I'm still very different to everyone else in the room, but now I feel happy and relaxed. I'm even more confident in myself. I don't need to say much because I know, I have an insight into disability that no-one else can possibly have and I am going to use my 'gift'. I'm really looking forward to the next academic year. I have so many ideas. I just want to get started.

PART 100

Blimey I am in a philosophical phase! I'm asking myself lots of questions. Here are my main puzzles. They are a bit chicken and egg!

1) Do you become an endurance athlete because you are physically and mentally resilient or does becoming an endurance athlete make you more physically and mentally resilient?

2) I consider that I am a better person because of Tooties, but was I already that person and Tooties brought me out or did Tooties actually make me into a better person?

3) Why doesn't a child who wants to be an astronaut when they grow up become an astronaut?

Answer 1 – After much consideration my answer is, "I don't know!"

111

Answer 2 – I don't mean did Tooties actually mess with my grey matter, I mean did the experience of Tooties and its accomplice Puss Pot change me, but for the better? Again after much consideration my answer is, "I'd like to think I was always the better person, but I'm not sure."

Answer 3 – I know, I know only a few people can go into space! The astronaut thing is really an analogy. What I'm really getting at is that when a child announces, 'When I grow up I want to be…' the adults usually just smile. Some even say, "You can be whatever you want to be darling." But how many actually mean that? Pretty soon, the adults in that child's life start to chip away at the dream either consciously or sub-consciously. They make decisions or say things that change the child's direction. In reality the adults are responsible for limiting the child's expectations. The child probably won't even realise this has happened because it happened so slowly and some may even believe they decided themselves!

But now I am that child. I want to be lots of things. I have lots of dreams or as grown-ups would say "aspirations". But already the adults in my life have started to try to put limitations on me. I even remember my surgeon saying to me a few days after my first op, "You may need to manage your expectations." I told him not to tell me what I can't do, only what I can! I know people are only being kind and cautious when they say "slow down, be careful," but I feel like they are stifling my enthusiasm. Waiting and being patient are all very well, but unless I try I will never know and that's what I believe happens to children. The would-be astronaut eventually agrees with Mummy that it is a 'silly idea' and does something else but do you know what? Someone has to be an astronaut! There might only be a few but they are out there floating in space. And that's my point I suppose. I am the child but I am also an adult. I can make my own decisions. I don't care if the other adults don't agree. The fact of the matter is, I have many dreams and aspirations and ultimately, I am in charge of my own destiny! Well God is, but I'm with Him!

PART 101

I have hit a speed bump in the road – no not literally, metaphorically! There doesn't appear to be an obvious physical reason for it, so we can only conclude it's my body's way of trying to tell me I need a bit of a rest. I've been having palpitations in my chest when I am running or cycling. It was really bad at my latest Park Run. I managed to keep going but that's probably because I am a bit stupid and definitely very stubborn! So I had to make a decision. Rest or race in my first open water event the next day? A good friend tried to appeal to the recovering patient in me but like Tim said, "There was no way we weren't getting up at stupid-o-clock the next morning for me to go and see what happens!" You see he knows I can't 'give in'.

PART 102 –
MY FIRST OPEN WATER RACE

Of course Tim was right. We got up very early and headed off to the race. When I registered I explained to the race director why I had entered the novice race. I thought she might be a bit confused as I had won my age-group at both her races last year. I also told her that if by any strange twist of fate I won, I wouldn't take the prize. She disagreed with me and said she would love it if I won and I would deserve to take the prize. I didn't win so it didn't matter, but I thought it was a fair thing for me to say and a lovely gesture on her part. But how did the race actually go? Once again the swim was the best bit. It was only 200m but we were in with the juniors and let me tell you – some of them can swim! So I lined up by the testosterone, adrenalin fuelled young men and kept out of trouble! They acted as a shield to the rest of the field and I emerged from the water in 2nd place. Very happy with that. However I soon realised that I had nothing in my legs and if I tried to push my 'heart thingy' kicked in and slowed me down even more. So I settled into a comfortable, slightly disappointing pace and hoped that by taking the bike section steady my legs would be happier on the 2.5km run. WRONG! I was very grateful it was only 2.5km. I finished 3rd and although the competitor in me was disappointed the rational me celebrated the positives. The main objective had been achieved: to see how my head felt in cold water. Ironically it didn't feel anything! Perhaps having a numb nut has its advantages! And I had finished! Despite feeling empty on the bike and horrible on the run I still crossed the finish line.

Part 103

I've had a bit of an epiphany this morning. I've been battling and experimenting with this 'heart flutter thingy' and I can't seem to find a pattern. But the strange thing is it doesn't happen when I swim. A friend suggested that Tim's psychological explanation might be right, that it was related to performance rather than fatigue. He thought I might be putting myself under a subconscious pressure to improve following my first race. His explanation was based on the fact that because my swim had gone really well, I wasn't thinking about it, but because the other two elements, particularly the run had been tough, subconsciously I was pushing myself too hard for my current level of fitness.

So where does the epiphany fit in? Well I was running along with LBM trying to decide what my breakdown should be (minutes/walk ratio not emotional!) and I started to think about how great it was that I now had a choice. I remembered that I had once written about my 'strong, beautiful' body and for the first time in a long time I actually believed it. Instead of thinking my overweight body was slowing me down and making me feel fat and sluggish I saw it in a different way. Not only had my body battled and beaten a brain tumour and an infection, it had done it in a record time and was still pushing me on. My body was allowing me to run with my dog in the sunshine. My body was enabling me to return to the work and the children I love. My body is an invincible machine. It didn't ever fail. It never let me down. It just needs time to repair. And maybe it was just coincidence, but for the first time in a couple of weeks, my heart didn't wobble!

PART 104

We have just returned from a wonderful over night stay with Team Abrams and boy did we fit a lot in! We went for a sea swim as soon as we arrived, which was hilarious because it was soooo cold, soooo rough and soooo eccentric! Who else other than a British triathlete would be seen semi-naked in a car park in a hail storm? Well, actually three British triathletes that's who!

After a lovely lunch we headed back to the beach for a few fartlek intervals. I started very conservatively but on the last effort I decided to give it some beans and see what my heart would do. It was fine. So my conclusion is that I was just having a bad patch. Perhaps my brain was sending out mixed messages? Who knows? I don't really care if it doesn't happen again!

After a lovely three course dinner with a large G & T and a good night's sleep we headed out on our bikes and I loved it. Some sections were really fast and I realised that this makes me very happy. Once again I felt grateful that my strong, beautiful body was allowing me to experience and enjoy this feeling again. I decided to share my thoughts with Tim and Team Abrams during our coffee stop. I confessed to feeling confused about how I look and feel at the moment and Sandra said she felt the same about her post-winter shape. She said she felt like a caterpillar when she looked at the rolls of fat on her tummy. I latched on to this analogy and joked that we were the 'hungry caterpillars' and we could munch and waddle together. But then Tim said something magical,

"But ladies, don't forget what caterpillars turn into – beautiful butterflies!"

And that's how I really do see it now. This is my caterpillar season. This is the summer when I eat and grow strong. Over the winter I will become a chrysalis and next spring I will emerge stronger, more powerful and even more resilient. I am going to be patient. I am going to absorb everything and I am going to be a true force of nature! You wait 'til you see my colourful wings and watch me fly!

PART 105

I've just returned from another philosophical bike ride! Being on my own should strike fear into me, but it doesn't. I find myself singing and thinking. The singing thing has only just started and I will explain more about that in a bit, but the thinking thing has always been there. I actually give most things a lot of thought and sometimes I get frustrated because people underestimate how deeply I do. Someone once suggested this is my fault because I have created a flippant persona who appears to breeze through life not giving much thought to anything. I vigorously disagree with this. Tim says I have the ability to think about nothing, which I do, but he also recognises that I think very earnestly about a lot things. Perhaps this has helped me to cope? Sometimes I think a lot, sometimes I don't think at all – balance!

So what provoked my thoughts today? A visit to my dear friend Sarah did. I haven't seen her since the week before my first operation, but as soon as I walked through the door six months melted away. We are completely different. We have vastly different backgrounds and lives, but what we do have in common is God. It was Sarah who exactly 10 years ago brought God into my life. And today I thanked her for that. As we sat in her kitchen laughing and drinking tea, we celebrated what our faith has given me. Sarah said she had prayed very hard for me but in her heart she always believed that my faith and my physical strength would see me through.

Now I appreciate that if you are a non-believer reading this you might say, "Sarah can't be that good a friend or Christian if she didn't visit you during your dark days and/or it was the doctors that saved you, not God." Well my response to you is this: I didn't judge Sarah because I know if she could have been with me she would. I knew she was carrying me in her heart and praying for me because we share a deep faith. I believe in her as she believes in me. Our friendship is pure. And as for the God versus doctors debate. Of course I know Mr P actually chopped my head open but I truly believe that God gave me the strength to relax and give Mr P and his team the best chance of success. I felt totally at ease when I went into theatre. I knew I would be looked after. If you don't 'believe' then this is probably very difficult to stomach – a load of religious bullshit some might say. But does it really matter to anyone else but me? Not really. As far as I'm concerned my unrelenting faith gave me hope – it kept my dreams alive. And now I am doing what I am doing, I can honestly say I am proof that miracles do happen!

Part 106

Why have I started to sing? When I was in hospital I decided I wanted to have a 'Life Party'. My idea was to invite all the people who I thought would have gone to my funeral. I wanted to celebrate my life with them and thank them for helping me through. As usual my idea started to grow and before long I wanted it to be a massive event which also included anyone I had met along the way. Then it became a fundraising event for my charity Brain Tumour Support. Then I decided I wanted live music etc etc.

As I write this at the end of May, the singing thing is still a BIG secret. Not even Tim knows what I have planned. At the party I will obviously thank everyone. I will read my Tooties poems and most people will weep, but I will find it easy. Many people have said I'm brave and courageous and as you know, I disagree. In fact I don't think I have ever been brave during my life. I have been confident and resilient, but not brave. So I thought "what can I do on the night that would require bravery? What would make me step so far outside my comfort zone even Tim would be amazed?" And then on the way back from London when we were listening to power ballads and I was killing them, it hit me – I could sing! I could stand up on the stage in front of 200 people and do something that a year ago I would have run away from. And not only could I sing, I could choose songs that really meant something.

I've had quite a few lessons with Lee now. I knew he was

the right teacher for me as soon as we spoke on the phone. He got me! And so I currently have a secret man in my life. Once a week I sneak over to Westbury by train or on my bike and I sing. My repertoire is growing. We began with 'Somewhere over the Rainbow'. It's a good training song but it also has pretty meaningful lyrics. I like it. I will start my gig with it. Now I am busy practicing my main pieces. Lee had a stroke of genius with one piece, which ironically led to the final piece. He said he had been singing it with his choir 'One Voice Community Choir'. OMG – it's perfect. As soon as I read it the words came alive and I knew that despite it being a very hard song to sing I just had to do it. I had to be brave and try. And the song…? It makes me feel excited just writing it: Whitney Houston's 'One Moment in Time'. Then I cheekily asked, "Lee do you think your choir would sing with me?" And guess what? They said yes!

And that's how I came across the song I am dedicating to Tim. I started to attend choir practice on Friday afternoons. Another top secret mission each week! I loved it and began to really enjoy singing and looked forwards to being with the group. They were all so friendly and welcoming and I now see them as friends. I can't believe that I have found something outside of sport that I absolutely adore. It excites me in a whole new way. It's another big positive that has come from my brain tumour!

The first time we sung my song for Tim, I nearly cried. The words were perfect. It was as if they had been written for me to sing to him. Once again I had chosen a difficult piece, but once again I felt completely motivated. I felt determined to learn it. Anything worth doing is never going to be easy and this is definitely worth doing! It's called 'Sometimes' and was inspired by the theme tune from the film 'Champions'. The lyrics are incredible and I can't wait to show Tim how much I love him.

PART 107

I'm reading another woman's autobiography about her battle with a disease that robbed her of her dreams. She was only 18 when she was diagnosed and so spends a lot of the book grieving for what she never achieved. This got me thinking again! Is my outlook different because we have very different temperaments or is it because I am so much older and have therefore achieved a lot already? And then I started to reminisce about all the wonderful sporting achievements I have had and the more I thought about them the more I realised I really have had a massive sporting career. I also realised that the common denominator throughout my inability to accept defeat until I am actually beaten. I have an absolute built-in desire to push and push until the final whistle and, ironically at this time with how I am feeling about my body and what I plan to do at my party, 'until the fat lady sings!'

I played women's football for over 20 years. I played in France at the student World Cup for Cardiff Institute of Education, I played for Wiltshire and Somerset and I also represented the South West Regional Team as well as playing for local clubs. I was never the most skilful of players but I was always very fit and I scored a lot of goals in the later stages of a match. I'd basically run the defence into the ground! In particular I remember two key matches. The first was a semi-final and we were three down at half time, but for me it wasn't over. I went out and smashed it. We won 4-3 and I scored a hat-trick with the winner on the final whistle. The second was a cup final. We were the underdogs. No-one believed we could win, but I did and I instilled this in my team. We played to our strengths – pump the ball down the pitch and let me chase it – again and again and again! We won 3-1 and I scored the perfect hat-trick: left foot, right foot, head. I still have the newspaper cutting for this game sitting proudly in my dining room. Sometimes I still think this was the most magical moment of my sporting career. The excitement and pride of turning when scoring and seeing 10 people running towards you so full of joy is difficult to explain. It's a team thing. It's pure adrenalin.

And then I found triathlon, quite by mistake actually. I'd started running and some friends persuaded me to do a sprint triathlon. I borrowed everything and can honestly say I absolutely hated riding a bike! But I did the race and despite a very slow T1 where I ran to my friends instead of my bike, I finished 5th. So in true Rachel Bown fashion I announced as I crossed the line, "Next year I am going to do a half Ironman and the year after that an Ironman." My friend said, "And I bet she does," and guess what? I did!

I came onto the GB Age Group scene when I decided to retire from football and see how good I could be at triathlon. I set myself the challenge of qualifying for

GB in my fortieth year. I decided that I had to qualify outright. A roll down wasn't good enough. So that's how it began. I finished 2nd in AG at The Dambuster and found myself going to Budapest. The dream had begun.

Since then my highest World ranking is 7th and I have won Silver and Gold at the Europeans. The Gold was a sprint finish and I won by one second. I thought I was winning and was just about to 'milk the crowd' when Tim screamed, "Sprint babe, she's in your age group!" So I did and we both collapsed over the line, but I had the gold gripped in my hand. And then last year in Kitzbuhel; again I grabbed what I wanted by one second – qualification for Geneva.

So you see I just can't give up. I will never believe it's over until I've actually crossed the line. And that's why I have now entered two qualifiers for next year's Europeans in Lisbon. My outlook has changed. A roll down is good enough this year. I don't think for one moment I will qualify outright. I will probably struggle to finish within the required 120% of the winner, but unless I race I won't know. You really do have to be in it to win it – and I'm still in it!!

PART 108

Thinking about cherished sporting memories took me back to the proudest day of my life – Day 5 of the Olympic Torch Relay 2012. This sounds a bit ridiculous but I didn't realise how proud I would be until it was actually happening! Two teachers at school nominated me independently and until this day they still squabble over whose nomination went through! I received an email to say I had been nominated and I had a one in a million chance of success. Then six months later I received another email to say I had been short-listed and had a one in 250,000 chance. Then a couple months later I had a third email to say I was in the final round and had a one in twelve chance and that's when it started to become real. That's when I realised I would be a tad disappointed if I wasn't selected. The email also said that the Torch Bearers would be notified on a certain date, so I counted down the days!

Then one morning I was getting ready for work when I was bombarded with text messages. Everyone who knew I had been nominated wanted to know if I'd been chosen. What were they on about? Apparently it was all over the news but I 'knew' it wasn't the right date. So I nonchalantly opened my laptop to see what all the fuss was about. Obviously people had got it all wrong! But they hadn't and there in black and white was my CONGRATULATIONS YOU ARE A TORCH BEARER email!

But do you know what? Even then I didn't feel overly excited. I was pleased to have been selected, but I didn't realise the sheer enormity of it until I was doing it. I don't think any of us did in the early days of the relay. Who could have predicted that the Torch Relay would capture the hearts and imaginations of the whole of Great Britain? What the relay did in spectacular fashion was to make every single spectator feel like they were part of the 2012 Olympics. The crowds were 20 deep in places and the noise was deafening. Kids were screaming and waving home-made flags. People came to watch us, the chosen few, run our 200m and celebrate with us. It was truly overwhelming. As we waited on the bus for our turn, we exchanged stories and that's when I felt very humble and very grateful. Some of my fellow Torch Bearers had done incredible things. They had raised thousands of pounds for charity, given hours and hours of their time to the community etc etc. What had I done? I'd just been me! I'd run a few races and taught lots of children with Special Educational Needs.

And then my name was called. I was number 50. My lit torch was handed to me and the bus stopped. The doors opened, the crowd erupted and the security officer said, "Rachel, this is your moment to shine!" My torch was already lit because I was the start of a new section and then I was running. It was a boiling hot day and it was actually quite difficult to balance the torch in one hand so that it didn't catch my hair on fire and wave with the other hand, whilst trying to absorb everything around me.

I had my own mini crowd waiting for me where the 'kiss' happened (that's what they called it when one torch lit the next). Mum and Dad, Auntie Ivy and Uncle Les, Tim's mum and sister, friends Charlotte and Bev, a group of sixth formers from school and of course Tim. Even the dogs were there as I remember!

Then we headed back to school for a special 'Torch Relay' tea party. Most of the children couldn't come to watch me because it was too far, but I could go to them.

They shared my special day with me and we loved it. I let the children run up and down the playground with the torch and every child (and probably adult!) had a photo taken with it.

My torch then did the rounds of schools and community groups all over Wiltshire and Somerset. It was bashed on tables and dropped a few times. It has chips and dents on it but I don't care. It has been loved and appreciated the way it should be. I was nominated because of the kids I work with so how could I ever deny them their 'moment to shine?!'

It was a wonderful day. I am part of Olympic history and that makes me feel very special. Thank you Anne and Rachel from school for nominating me – it doesn't matter which one of you wrote the 'winning' application!

PART 109

I'd been really excited about my first big race, so why was I crying on my way to the Nottingham Sprint Triathlon? Was I scared? No. Was I worried I'd be out classed in a European Qualifier? No. So why was I crying? I suddenly felt overwhelmed and grateful. Although I had already raced locally, this felt different. The big stage is where I believe I belong and I suppose a little bit of me still couldn't process that I was actually going to be back on it.

I had a brilliant day. I love the atmosphere and really enjoy catching up with friends I only see at the big events.

One lady even burst into tears when she saw me walk into transition. I received lots of hugs and once again people told me I was inspirational. The reality is being around them inspires me and never more so than that day.

I came away feeling that I can achieve anything and that with time I will be stronger and fitter than ever. I finished exactly 115% behind the winner which was also exactly 115% behind my winning time two years ago. Remember Mr P's 20% target? Well I've already smashed it by 5% in a month! So although I realise that my rate of improvement will slow down and even plateau at times, I really can't see why with my renewed passion and excitement for life I can't create new limits or rather, remove my limits. The child in me wants to be an astronaut!

PART 110

Today I feel like I've been given the biggest piece of cake I could wish for and then the baker has run towards me with a big dollop of creamy icing and spread it thickly all over the top. Now I know this wouldn't be good for my ever expanding waistline but as it's just an analogy I can enjoy the calorie free version instead! As if being well wasn't good enough. As if training again wasn't good enough. As if racing wasn't good enough. As if Geneva wasn't good enough. Are you getting the gist yet? As if everything that is happening wasn't good enough, this morning I received an email from the GB Sprint Team Manager asking me if I wanted to be my country's captain in Geneva! OMG! She said she had been following my progress and thought I was an inspiration and would be perfect for the role. What an honour! So I gave it some thought – all of a micro second and immediately responded with a simple "YES PLEASE! I can't wait!" answer. I am over the moon. It really is the icing on the cake. This is one of the proudest days of my life. I know I can do a good job and in particular assist the first timers. I want them to enjoy and savour the event as much as possible. Who could possibly have seen this a few months ago? I really do believe my future and my comeback are written in the stars!

Part 111

With just under five weeks until this book finishes, I'm beginning to re-read it and 'tidy it up'! I am so glad I documented everything because although I have very clear memories of most of it, some things were sure to have been forgotten and that would be a shame. What I am pleased to have read is that as I've moved through the process I've healed and accepted what has been happening very quickly. In the beginning I worried I wouldn't be the person I wanted to be. I hoped I would be strong, but I wasn't sure. I didn't know how Tim would cope with me if I wasn't coping and I worried that at the end of it all I would be free of Tooties but also minus a partner. I wondered if everything was bluff and bravado and that underneath it all I would turn out to be one big fake. Did I say positive things and make jokes in the hope that if I said them enough, eventually I would believe them myself? And the answer is… NO! Reading back confirms what I now know. I was put on this earth to make a difference, but not in the way I had planned. God's plan was different to mine. I always felt like a big fish, but now I know I'm a cuddly shark! I don't have a little pond to swim around in, I have a never-ending ocean and I'm excited to see how far I can swim!

Part 112

As I re-read this book I am also reminded about how hard and upsetting it has been to watch my mum and dad suffer. I've agonised about just how honest I should be in my editing, because I am very aware of how brutal some of my entries might appear. I don't want either of them to read this book and feel ashamed or angry. But the bottom line is I did feel all those things and I did experience those situations. What I wrote was from my heart and it was real. It did happen.

But what I desperately want them to do is see past those entries and see the bigger picture. I hope they don't get halfway through, slam the book down and give me both barrels. I hope they can read to the end so that they realise this book is just a moment in time. Yes, some may argue that it is a hideous moment in time, but as you know, I view it differently. This year has been the year that truly cemented the Bown family together. We are only a very small unit and yet we coped with levels of trauma that most people could never even imagine. We never wavered in our love for each other and none of us ever thought about giving up on anyone. Mum and I were so poorly at times, that Richard and Dad had to make very swift, dynamic decisions and they never got it wrong. I am very proud of us. We made it through and although we will probably always have battle scars, we still have each other. We are triumphant. We are winners. We survived and we are the Bown family!

PART 113

In three weeks' time we will be on our way to Geneva. How am I feeling? Well my phased return to work hasn't really happened, so I am a bit weary, have a sore throat and I've burnt my lip on some pasta – now that's what you call a proper sporting injury! Really though, I'm fine. I know I'm doing too much, but my priority list isn't vertical, it's horizontal and so basically I am trying to do everything. Being with the kids at school and organising stuff across the area makes me happy. It's not selfless because I get a lot of satisfaction and pleasure from it. So when people say, "You've got to think of yourself," I am. My emotional well-being is embedded in my job. As I've said before I am not a workaholic, but I will always do my best for the kids.

In terms of the actual race, I am feeling very relaxed. Hopefully I can squeeze into my tri-suit by then! For me this event is so different. I do intend to do my best on the day. I will push as hard as I can. You will still see my race face, but you will also see my biggest ever grin. I don't have any pressure. I have no expectations. I will captain my country with pride and race freely. I plan to cross the finish line with a salute to God. I will then turn back towards the course and take a bow. I will have won my race!

PART 114

I've now been to two European Championship 2016 qualification races. Remember the first one was Nottingham and I finished 115% behind my age-group winner. Well at Southport I smashed that percentage and I didn't even execute a good race! I pretty much committed every school girl error in the book! I forgot my swim hat, so Tim went to get it and I asked a stranger to zip my wetsuit up. This had consequences later. The swim was a real fight, which I don't mind but in parts it was ridiculous. It appears that I can sight a buoy better with one eye than many women can with two! Then when I got out I discovered my suit had been secured too well and I couldn't find the zip strap. Pretty frustrating! Then I couldn't find my bike. I actually stood still by a rack and shouted, "Where's my bike?" – twice! I realised my run shoes etc weren't there either – hmmm, I was in the wrong place! The bike course was so windy I held on to my aero bars for dear life and hoped I didn't get blown off. It's the only time I've ever been happy with my extra weight! But then came the ultimate error, I went the wrong way on the run! Now the fact that the route was one lap of the lake should have meant this was impossible, but not for me (and many others as it transpired) and I ran straight past the turning to the finish. Let's just say I wasn't exactly relaxed and smiling as I crossed the line. My main concern was that this mistake would cost me a place in Lisbon.

When I saw the results I burst into tears. I've never cried at a race before. I'd finished 5th. I cried because I was so shocked I had finished so high up and because for the first time in nearly a year I had proof that I can be as good as I was. I was 3rd fastest in the swim and 2nd fastest on the bike. I was 1st in T1 and 2nd in T2. I have a lot of work to do on my running, but as that was my strength pre-Tooties, I'm confident it will come back. It's a year on Tuesday that I was told there was something seriously wrong me and I needed tests. The specialist told me I may never exercise again, let alone race. That anniversary makes today even more poignant! In real terms my finishing percentage is now just 107%. I stand a chance of sneaking an automatic qualification and if I don't get that, my chances of a roll down place are very high. Let's put it this way, I'm planning my trip to Lisbon!

PART 115

Another visit to the Eye Hospital has pretty much confirmed what I have always thought. My eye probably won't track back round and I won't regain any vision. The registrar (bless him!) looked very uncomfortable when I asked him the direct questions and visibly relaxed when I told him I had accepted my situation and that he wouldn't upset me. He is now filling in my forms for British Blind Sport. When they are completed I will send them off for classification – am I blind enough? That's the question!

PART 116

The anniversaries are beginning to roll in now! It's a year since D-Day! At exactly 2.50pm on Wednesday 2nd July I received the phone call that changed my life. I've been unexpectedly emotional already and it's only 6.15am! I think that this is the first time that what I've been through has really dawned on me! I know that sounds ridiculous, but a year ago today was really the start of the rest of my life. And it's also the first time I've thought about 'it' coming back. Perhaps reliving that day has made realise how awful it was? Perhaps I have been on a roller coaster of coping and not really considered the extent of what has happened to me and those around me? All I know is that for the first time I have googled my condition. I have dared to look at what the average prognosis is and what the realistic chances of me having to go through all this again are. I have also delved into the world of radiation therapy and what it does and how it can affect you.

So what are my conclusions? They are actually pretty simple: today I feel great. Today I feel excited about everything I have to look forward to. I have regained my 'normality' quicker than anyone has ever seen before and for that I am grateful. I'm not stupid or unrealistic but that doesn't mean I am being pessimistic or negative. I understand that I'm likely to be affected again at some point in my life, but at what point no-one knows. I can't sit around micro-analysing myself every second of every day – I've got too much to do and too much life to live. Tumours are boring!

Part 117

Historically this has always been a very, very busy time of year for me at work. This year has been no exception. I didn't feel under any pressure to organise lots of fun

PE stuff, but I wanted to. Again I didn't want the kids to miss out because I had been poorly. If I could get it organised, it was happening! I am exhausted, but it was sooo worth it. The Sporting Champions Assembly that you read about towards the start of this book happened again, only this year it was even bigger and better. The problem for me was that it happened on the anniversary of D-Day and this meant I just couldn't say all the things I wanted to say out loud. When I tried my mind either went blank or I could feel myself welling up. My solution was to say what I felt on FB and I think my message was heard. In summary, I am motivated by my world to be the best I can be so that those around me can be the best they can be. I completely understand how what I do affects others. I work hard to give the children at my school the PE opportunities they deserve. I watch them smile and jump about as they collect their trophies or see their picture in the presentation, but what I also see is the look on their parent's faces. Many parents will never have dreamed about a moment like this. They may never have thought that their child would be capable enough or that their world could mirror mainstream education. The pride on their faces and the tears that they shed give me goosebumps. Of course their child is able. Of course their child should have the opportunity. And I am proud to be the facilitator. I am proud to say I made them cry!

PART 118

I am now being told daily that I am an 'inspiration' and of course I am very flattered and very grateful for such lovely comments. People say I must be very strong and very motivated and that they really admire me. But all I am is me! I'm happy to be seen in this way, but I never want anyone to think I coveted it. I will never stand in front of anyone and announce "I am motivational because…" Yes I want to do more public speaking. I want to set up a website and promote positivity, but my way might not be your way, I get that.

PART 119

I am now a week away from finishing this little gem! So many people have said they would like to read it, hopefully they will cough up a tenner plus to do so! It's Geneva week! Yes, the big event is nearly here. One more day at school and then the party begins.

PART 120

Three days until Geneva/ three days 'til the end of this book!

I'm sat in the car at Dover waiting for Tim to sort our transfer across the water. You see our lives were never designed to be uneventful – our ferry company has disbanded! Oh yeah and the ferry workers are refusing to get off the ferries in Calais and we can't go through the Euro tunnel at the moment because some immigrants are blocking it! I do have a solution, tell both groups that unless they move I will be paying them a visit. Apparently I am motivational and inspiring so I'm sure I can help them to change their minds!

My offer has not been accepted, probably because someone has actually died in the tunnel! We are now in the Channel Tunnel queue. It's only a four hour delay so we can have lots of fun sitting in the car waiting! On the plus side I am resting, just a bit more than I planned.

The time has passed quite quickly (I slept mostly) and we have had a good run through France. When we got to the Swiss border the 'road tax collector' tried to con us. He wanted 50 euros cash but when Tim paid on the card it was only 40! Nice con if you can do that 10 times a day. But despite our good progress we haven't made the apartment check-in deadline so we are having to spend another 60 euros on a motorway hotel.

Now we are finally in Geneva but we couldn't find the long stay car park and the Internet in our apartment has failed. Tim has also had a few issues buying some groceries and we are both exhausted.

But this trip to date has made me realise how differently I am approaching this race. Historically I would be very, very anxious. The catalogue of errors would have upset me and the demons would be sat firmly on my shoulders chattering away. When I had a quick swim the water was cold but I know I can swim 750m in or out of my wetsuit. I don't really care. When I went on the bike recce I was last up the big hill. I don't really care. This is probably the wrong terminology, because I do really care, but not about logistics and race course stuff that is completely out of my control. All of this trivia is just that – trivia.

I am here. I have achieved something that six months

ago was just a dream. Today I will sit with my team in our group photo and smile proudly and then tomorrow morning I will pull on my GB kit and line up alongside the best 45-49 female triathletes in Europe and I will race!

PART 121 – RACE DAY

When Mr P said I may lose my competitive edge I didn't understand what he meant. I thought he must mean 'physically' because I couldn't imagine that my extreme competitive nature could ever be over ridden by anything! He had explained I may always feel like I've already won and that that feeling could take my 'edge'. I disagreed at the time and as all my races in the build up to Geneva have shown, I still want to push my own personal limits and see how high up the pack I can finish.

But I did always say that Southport was my A race because that impacted and set up next year. Geneva was always going to be my party race. Tim thought I would surprise myself but I had a different feeling. It wasn't a bad feeling. I didn't think something horrible was going to happen. In fact I thought the course was great, but something was different.

However I wasn't prepared for what that 'different' would look like! For the first time in my sporting career I couldn't focus on what was actually happening. I really did only see a bigger picture. As soon as I stepped into the water all my nerves disappeared and I was just going for a swim! The gun went and I happily settled into a comfortable pace. I didn't fight for space and I didn't attempt to draft off anyone faster. I thought about how lovely the water was and how happy I was to be enjoying it. I had a great spot in transition and got out of my wetsuit easily, but I still didn't run out of T1 like a scalded cat, I took my time. On the bike I actually sang out loud for most of the first lap (there were three) practicing for my party! On the horrible hill that everyone was so worried about, I spun up in my lowest gear and thanked the spectators for their support. On the run I smiled and thanked people. What I realised right from the start was that if I pushed to my limits one of two things would happen and both would be wrong.

1) I could push push push in every aspect, but my fitness could only give me so much in return. The effort: reward ratio wasn't in my favour. I would probably have finished higher up the results, but I would have missed out on a better experience.

2) I could push push push and find myself having to walk on the run or worse find myself in the back of an ambulance. I recognised how selfish this would be. To put Tim and my family through that would be wrong. I didn't know how my body would cope in the heat, so to test it without caution was unfair and irresponsible.

So what was this 'different' experience? It was one of reflection actually. The reason I couldn't focus was that I felt like I was having an out of body experience. Throughout the race I replayed the last year in my head just like it was a film. Of course I was a fab leading lady! So glamorous throughout! At certain points I remembered Kitzbuhel and how differently I approached and attacked the course, but mostly I remembered how poorly I had been and how hurt I had felt. I saw myself lying in hospital, not knowing what my future looked like. At times I just couldn't see how I would ever compete again.

So I genuinely smiled and enjoyed every second and I now realise part of me didn't want it to end. I literally wanted to savour every moment. When I stepped off the Olympic Torch bus the official said, "Rachel, this is your moment to shine," and this is exactly how I felt during the race. I was shining and I was winning. Exactly six months earlier I was rushed back into hospital for my second operation and here I was racing in the sunshine. It was surreal because I knew that apart from a little bit (well a lot actually, but let's not dwell on that!) of timber, in my sunglasses and race kit I looked the same on the outside, but I knew how different I now am on the inside – both physically and emotionally.

As I turned into the finishing funnel I was already close to tears. I took the Union flag from Tim and gave him a kiss. I crossed the finishing line and as promised, I turned back and raised my arms as a salute to God and everyone who had loved and supported me. And then I cried. I had never felt more alive!

So did I make Mr P's 'extraordinary' percentage? No I didn't. I was way off it. But I had achieved it when it really mattered – at the Euro 2016 qualifiers and I'm pretty sure no-one has ever achieved what I achieved today. So I am going to say I am 'extraordinary'!

PART 122 – WHAT'S NEXT?

I've got one eye on the future (pun intended!) but not the long term future. What I've learnt this past year is that the future may never come. I don't know if my tumour will rear its ugly self again. I don't know if one of the other little invaders may decide to 'grow up', but I do know how I want to live my life. I will seize every opportunity, enjoy what I have and make the most of every day. If you smile at the world, it really does smile back. I really have learnt that it's not about dodging the storm, it's about dancing in the rain – naked if you want to!

Am I full of cheesy quotes and clichés – hell yes! And why not?

THE FINAL PART!

Believing in yourself really can make dreams come true. Be that astronaut. Release the butterfly within!

Thank you for reading about my year. I hope you have enjoyed it and remember – we really do have two lives, but the second only begins when we realise we only have one! God bless xx

Characters I encountered along the way!

I spent a total of five weeks in hospital and during that time I came across or heard many different people. Here are a few:

Shuffler- named because he continuously shuffled up and down the corridor in his slippers. I never actually saw him!

Doris- this lovely old lady was on the stroke ward. She would cry when the nurse took her blood pressure because the cuff hurt. The nurses were always very kind and patient with her. I never saw Doris, but for some reason I cared.

Crazy Frog- remember that irritating techno track from 2000 and something? Well, this guy could drown out any DJ! Obviously he was very poorly, but so was I. In the end I asked to be moved. I never actually saw him!

Sex Pest- OMG this was funny. So there I am in HDU when a lady and her husband (both in their sixties) came onto the ward. She laid on the bed and said, "I'm sorry you missed your Friday treat."
He replied, "But you forget, we had a nice swim."
"I don't mean that treat," she said reaching for his crutch. He jumped back and said, "I'm going to leave now because you are becoming inappropriate."

"Why don't you get in bed with me?" she persisted. "I know you want to, I can feel it in your trousers!"

"That's my phone. I'm going now." He practically sprinted off the ward!

When a male nurse came to help the lady change into a night gown she said to him, "At least you want to see my body. I offered it to my husband and he wasn't interested!" I immediately messaged Tim – there was a sex pest on my ward!

Chequers Man- he walked past me many times and every time he said, "Fancy a game of chequers?" as he held out his chess/draughts board. Each time I replied, "Sorry my head hurts and I'm very tired." Then one time it dawned on me how lonely he was, so I agreed to one game, explaining I hadn't played since I was a small girl with my grandad. We played and he won. He chatted about his condition and explained that his family wouldn't visit because it was Christmas. I'm glad I had a game with Chequers Man and shame on his family!